The Current of Spirituality

The Current

by

TEMPLEGATE, Publisher

of Spirituality

Hubert van Zeller

Springfield, Illinois

© 1970 by Hubert van Zeller
All rights reserved
Library of Congress Catalog Card Number 74—136461
SBN 87243-048-0
Printed in the United States of America

*When ten thousand things are viewed in their oneness
we are able to return them, and we ourselves return with them,
to their Origin, and there together
we remain where we have always been.*

                                                Sen T'sen

Foreword

Serious Christians everywhere are talking about the Church of the future, Church renewal, the flowering of fraternal love, the loosening of bonds which have held religion so tightly for centuries. The re-awakening of concern is well and good, but there is little corresponding interest in prayer. Indeed the evidence points the other way. While we hear a certain amount about prayer being a sort of witness, we do not often see people praying. We may admit the value of a "new awareness" of social responsibility, respect for the individual conscience, and the need for change in forms of worship, but something is still lacking. Unless there emerges the worship of God from the heart, collectively and personally, the energy expended may well be wasted. Zeal for new expressions of service is not itself service, and certainly not a substitute for the life of

Foreword

the Spirit. While the Churches are making a great deal of fuss over theological, moral, structural, and liturgical reforms, and while ideas on every conceivable religious subject are being aired, little attention is being given to the actual life of the Spirit.

We tend to think of rival spirits at work, of action in competition with contemplation. In a materialist world, action is seen to win hands down. It is the old business of Martha or Mary — as though it were an option — rather than allowing the works of Martha to emerge from the spirit of Mary. The test lies not in the opinion which emerges but in the kind of faith which shows itself when people pray. Any fool can decide whether or not he likes certain existing or proposed reforms, whether he agrees or disagrees with a liberal interpretation of Scripture, and the like, but it takes real generosity to get on with the work of deep, personal, day-to-day prayer — an element in the Church's life that has largely been neglected in favor of controversy. (You have only to look at publishers' book lists for evidence of that.) The growing popularity of religious features on television is not necessarily a sign of spiritual life; nor do discussion groups take its place. Patting oneself on the back for holding the views one does — and getting together with others to congratulate them for being in agreement — can be just one more way of avoiding the life of the Spirit, the life to which we are divinely called.

The premise of this book is that the life of Christians

Foreword

should have true Christian spirituality at the center, whatever the circumstances. Whether our concern is the life of prayer itself, or ecumenism, or Church renewal, or Christian activism, without the actual work of prayer it will all be in vain. We are called to be like Christ, to know the will of God, but we cannot do it by simply relying upon what we have heard, or by catching hold of the latest theory or interpretation; we can do it only by allowing God to work in us and through us, which means giving Him the space and time that He needs for that work — and that, of course, is what spirituality is all about.

Hubert van Zeller

Shimdda Hir
Penrhyn Bay
Llandudno
North Wales
July 1, 1970

Contents

CHAPTER 1	*THE BASIC PRINCIPLE*	*13*
CHAPTER 2	*THE CURRENT OF SPIRITUALITY*	*23*
CHAPTER 3	*DEEPER IDENTIFICATION*	*33*
CHAPTER 4	*AN UNFORTUNATE SIDE EFFECT*	*39*
CHAPTER 5	*WHAT THE OUTCOME SHOULD BE*	*53*
CHAPTER 6	*WHY MAN SHRINKS FROM IT*	*63*
CHAPTER 7	*CAN IT CHANGE ITS COURSE?*	*73*
CHAPTER 8	*COMMUNICATION*	*87*
CHAPTER 9	*SUFFERING*	*91*
CHAPTER 10	*HAPPINESS*	*101*
CHAPTER 11	*FAILURE*	*111*
CHAPTER 12	*ACTUAL SET PRAYER*	*119*
CHAPTER 13	*MATURITY*	*129*
CHAPTER 14	*FREEDOM*	*139*
CHAPTER 15	*WORK*	*145*
CHAPTER 16	*RENEWAL*	*155*
CHAPTER 17	*SUMMING UP*	*165*

1

The Basic Principle

If someone stopped you in the street and asked, "Are you like Christ?" your feelings would probably be mixed. First you would be shocked at the mention of Christ by a perfect stranger; then you would feel annoyed at being subjected to such a personal question; and then you would begin to wonder what sort of answer you could honestly give. "I'm afraid I'm not," you might say, or "I would like to be." Or you might ask in turn, "Is anybody?" Yet to be like Christ is the first purpose of the Christian: it comprises every other religious duty; it is not an impractical ideal: Christ is God made imitable. While your interrogator might be guilty of poor manners, you could hardly fault him on his evangelism. As a fellow Christian, he is not strictly a stranger to you; he too is meant to be like Christ; both of you are members of Christ's body, and it ought not to be

The Current of Spirituality

shocking for one member to want to know how another member is getting on in fulfilling his first purpose.

The significance of spirituality cannot be evaluated apart from Christ. As He has opened to us the supernatural world, so it is only by explicit reference to Him that the reality of the supernatural world can be revealed to us. Spirituality is not an abstraction but an identification. By relating ourselves consciously and deliberately to the Christ-life we come to enjoy the fullest development of both natural and spiritual life which is possible to man. Whoever says that he can practise the Christian virtues without formulating his allegiance to Christ is talking nonsense. Without Christ there are no Christian virtues; there are only good habits. Christ is the alpha and omega, the beginning and the end.

The primary condition then is a belief in the inter-personal relationship between the Christian and Christ. Before you can get anywhere in the spiritual life you have to be convinced that such a relationship is possible and that it is open to *you*. Whether or not it brings with it a comfortable assurance of eternal life to be spent in Christ's company is neither here nor there; all you have to concern yourself with is trying to unite your whole living self with the whole living self of Christ. You are alive; Christ is alive. You are not pledging yourself to a dead hero, but to someone who is as alive as you are. Unless the availability of such a relationship is admitted, unless Christ is thought of at all times as a living, accessible being, it is no good

The Basic Principle

talking about Christian spirituality.

The fact that the living Christ is divine may make Him seem remote, but the fact that He is also human should bring him close. For most of us, however, it is not the doctrine that is the trouble. We accept the notion of "two natures in one person" because that is what Christianity teaches us — the doctrine is provided; the difficulty lies in the bringing of our spirituality into harmony with the doctrine. That is where care must be taken to avoid placing too much reliance on "spiritual experience." The concept of spirituality refers to subjective rather than to objective perceptions, but it does not mean that spiritual development is really a matter of developing inner appetites regardless of their relationships to objective reality. In the Christian understanding of faith one is not being led to satisfy himself on fancies, but to continue in a search which has to do with facts, and fact here is the living reality of Christ.

Love is the cause and crown of everything, but the key to everything is faith. An often forgotten fact of faith is that mysteries are not the only material on which it has to function. It must act on actualities as well. Nowhere is this more clearly revealed than in the life of Christ; in the historical fact of His years as a man among men, and as God among men. Faith was just as necessary to the people of Palestine as it is to Christians now. The problem was not made easier by being able to see and hear our Lord; if anything, it was made more difficult. The evidence of the

The Current of Spirituality

senses can, in any age, stand in the way of the evidence of the spirit. There was to be no absolute proof or there would have been no absolute faith. The reality of Jesus, God and man, was there, just as the reality exists for us today, but there was no compulsion about the acceptance of that reality.

Faith was expressed by the wise men and shepherds at the time of Christ's infancy. It was revealed by Anna and Simeon in the temple. Elizabeth made her act of faith before the birth of John, and so, eventually, did her husband Zachary. John himself recognized Christ and preached His messianic identity even from his prison. Apart from His family and the immediate circle of His followers who might have been expected to know who He was, Christ's contemporaries were not called upon to make an explicit act of faith until He publicly proclaimed Himself to be Son of God and the Messiah. Bear in mind that in the following we are not considering a mystical experience but the realistic appraisal of an historical fact.

Consider the circumstances: A village workman, a provincial young man with no rabbinical degrees, claiming to be not only the holy one foretold by the prophets but holiness itself: Yahweh's human projection of Himself. We know what happened: "He came to His own, and His own received him not." The people had looked for one kind of incarnation — God had arranged for another. They believed the word when it was written in the pages of revelation but not when the "word was made flesh." The reason they

The Basic Principle

misunderstood the coming of the Messiah was not only that they expected a religious nationalist, and, closer to home, that He was too familiar a figure in His Nazareth setting, but, more subtly, because they lacked the spirituality which would have afforded them finer sensititivy and greater flexibility. They did not see because they were looking in the wrong direction; they were looking in the wrong direction because their spiritual life was bent the wrong way.

The puzzling thing about it is that some rather unexpected people did see. Since there is no mention of divine illuminations where they were concerned we conclude that they had laid themselves open to the spirit in a way which others — more professionally "spiritual" — had not. Why did Zaccheus recognize Christ's claims and the high priest not? Why did Mary Magdalen see Christ as her Saviour and Simon the Pharisee not? Why did the Roman centurion, a woman of Canaan and another of Samaria, and a thief believe; and most of the scribes, rabbis, pharisees, members of the Sanhedrin, and religious leaders generally did not? The answer must be in the receptivity of the unlikely people; and the likely people, who might have been expected to pray, did in fact not pray. By genuine prayer their spiritual capacity — the ability to recognize truth when it is presented — would have been enlarged. They saw only what was outwardly presented and could not bring themselves to take a deeper look.

Even among those who are close to Christ the hazard

The Current of Spirituality

persists. They see Him so clearly in one form that they miss Him when He comes to them in another. That is why He told His disciples, "Unless I go, the Holy Spirit will not come to you." At the end of St. Mark's account of the Gospel there is a significant verse which tells how Christ "appeared to them in another shape." Between the Resurrection and the Ascension He appeared variously as a traveller, a gardener and as a man standing on a beach. On each of those occasions, He was not immediately recognized. His friends who had known Him almost too well, had to unlearn what they knew if they were to meet Him in the newer revelations of Himself. "Touch me not, for I am not yet ascended to my father." With the coming of the Holy Spirit the challenge of faith is seen to be on a new plane. From then on the words of our Lord to St. Thomas, "Blessed are they that have not seen but have believed," take on deeper meaning.

A moral may be drawn therein respecting the changes taking place in the Christian churches of today. The Christ we knew, the Christ who conformed to former, familiar specifications, the Christ who spoke to us in accents which could not be mistaken, is appearing all over the world in different forms. Just as after the Resurrection He changed yet remained the same, so now in the upheavals of our own time He appears differently but He is, in fact, the same. Nothing but our own spirituality will show us the authentic Christ. In an age of nearly as many false prophets as true, we must know where to look and be generous enough to follow what faith tells us we see.

The Basic Principle

Let us return to the opening paragraph and reexamine the three random answers to the question, "Are you like Christ?" They are of one piece: everybody can be like Christ if he wants to. The principle of the Christ-life is an active reality in all Christians. The reason it is not more self-evident in many Christians is that so few really believe it. They give a nominal assent to the doctrine but do not put their potential into practice; or they restrict their identity with Christ to some particular aspect of life: to suffering perhaps, or to the forgiveness of injuries. Surely the point is complete identification — right down the line. Christ has His own life, and in it has an infinite happiness. In the Father's plan, and therefore in His, you and I have a place, as with two chemicals in a test-tube which are meant to mix. Christ can manage without you and me, but we cannot manage without Christ. We have to mix with Him and with one another; with Him first, and then with one another. Love is the dynamic quality which brings the substance out of the academic test-tube into the world of everyday experience, but there has to be faith before the action occurs. Spirituality as outlined so far means exactly this: faith, hope and charity. Nothing very new as a moral code and Christian ethic, but absolutely vital as a way of achieving life of Christ.

Is anyone really living the life of Christ? We do not know, and can never know. For my own part, I feel that many more people are living it than would outwardly appear. I refer not only to those who minister to the sick in obscure and anonymous service or those who are them-

The Current of Spirituality

selves living lives of patient sacrifice; I am thinking of quite wordly people who would be astounded to find themselves thought of as spiritual or religious, who answer to the straightforward evangelical summons. Surely if they want Christ, however inadequate they may feel about living up to His ideal when He manifests Himself to them, they are in the tradition of Anna and Simeon. In a sense, they are exposing themselves to fuller revelation. They need not say "I shall leave all and follow him." One thing at a time: they should be able to say, "If he grants me the grace to take the step I shall do whatever He has in mind, even if He asks me to leave all and follow Him."

Wanting to be like Christ is the first thing. It is the token offering which He seeks. Given it, He can build something which can in a very real way can be in His own image and likeness. Without it, religion is likely to be an academic affair, cold and impersonal. Without it, spirituality may as well be Buddhist, Confucian or Hindu. For the Christian there is only one Way and Truth and Life, and though he may respect other ways, relative truths, and all life, Christ is the only way, the only guide. No Christ, no spirituality; although to some degree every Christian has his stake in spirituality because in some degree every Christian is living the life of Christ.

The degree to which the Christian chooses to identify his life with the life of Christ will inevitably mark the degree to which his life reflects the life of Christ. He will bear in mind that Christ was accused of keeping bad

The Basic Principle

company, of being a drunkard, of being mad, of being possessed of a devil, of violating the Sabbath, of arrogance in preaching against the establishment, of bearing witness to Himself in His claim to be God, and consequently of being a blasphemer and an impostor. Very few Christians will be found to take on even a pale reflection of all that. Though not seriously considered to be mad, most of us are sometimes thought to be peculiar. Though not openly charged with being impostors and traitors, most of us have put up with being called hypocrites, with being accused of double-dealing, with being guilty of disloyalty towards our particular society or our commitments. Experiences of that sort can and should be related to the infinitely more painful experience of Christ, but does not reliving the life of Christ in the setting of the twentieth century mean something more than that?

If the idea of Christ as the exemplar is to be more than a vague and inspiring doctrine, is He not more than just a symbol for Christians, a phenomenon without implications? Is our identification with Christ nothing more than a piece of fiction which happens to come true only on inescapable occasions? Or is the life of Christ something at once practical and spiritual in its contemporary application, something to which in his ordinary life the Christian may find a parallel? If you are speaking of the spiritual current in the world, there it is. The current of spirituality runs through every century of history and its source is Christ. "If any man thirst, let him come to me and drink . . . out from me shall flow fountains of living water . . . no man

The Current of Spirituality

comes to the Father save by me ... learn of me ... the Paraclete, the Holy Spirit, whom the Father will send in my name, he will teach you all things ... I go away and I come unto you ... abide in me and I in you ... without me you can be nothing."

2

The Current of Spirituality

This book is meant not so much for beginners as for those who have begun and who need to be encouraged to begin again. Unless you are prepared to renew your purpose day by day, you tend to slacken off and forget the ideal that you have set yourself. Not only can you grow stale, tacitly denying your original surrender to the action of God, but you can also persuade yourself that no more is required than what you are now giving to God, that in the nature of the case you cannot feel the same freshness which the spiritual life once held for you, and that whether or not you have been negligent in the matter there is nothing you can do about it.

The point to be noted at the outset is that the current of spirituality is always there, always on the move below

The Current of Spirituality

the surface, and that what you have to do is meet up with it, and, constantly correcting your course, see that you do not lose it. There are times when its movement feels strong enough to carry you without further effort on your part, as there are times when you feel you are doing all the work while the current has submerged so deeply as to be of no assistance. That is where faith and an elementary knowledge of the ways of the spirit obtain. You know if your progress is made by a power not your own, that you are being carried along. The current never stops; it is only the recognition of it that falters.

One of the most common misconceptions is to imagine that having once stepped out of the stream, you cannot at any moment step in again. Neither stupidity nor sin alters the course of the current: you can rejoin the flow whenever you desire. The saints are not those who are seen triumphantly riding the waters whatever the pull against them; more often they are those who are unsure of themselves and their location, who feel themselves to be floundering in whirlpools which rob them of their sense of direction, who doubt their ability to remain afloat another minute, yet who hold tenaciously to the conviction that God who has put them where they are remains in control of the waters.

To think differently about the call to union with God (and it is union with God that spirituality is all about), leads only to discouragement and, at worst, despair. It is one thing to admit your inconstancy, your inability to hold

The Current of Spirituality

to the original plan of total surrender, and quite another to turn away, saying you have missed your chance. You may have missed a chance, and you may have made things harder for yourself by so doing, but the beauty of it is that there are chances being given all the time. That you must believe or you will never get anywhere: it is the first meaning of trust — not trust in your power to recover a lost position, but in God; not in a miracle which will alter your nature, remove a temptation, or provide a solution to a particular problem, but trust in God. A spirituality which cannot produce trust is not true spirituality. Self-assurance and wishfulness may make for a trust of sorts, but it is not the trust which goes with authentic spirituality.

Nothing is easier than to examine yourself in the matter (it is a mistake to imagine that your spirituality is something which cannot be tested except by somebody else): all you have to do is to give honest answers to such questions as, Do I really believe that God alone is to be relied upon in the directing of my life, in providing the circumstances best suited to that direction, in giving me everything necessary? Or do I hold to the idea that if I keep my wits about me I can carve out my own kind of life? Do I look wistfully at conditions of life other than my own in which I would be able to give God a better service than I am now giving? Have I a sneaking feeling that by making up my mind and taking a firm line for once, by the force of my will, I could overcome this or that bad habit? Where problems of others are concerned, do I rely upon my persuasive powers, my native wisdom, my charm, my

The Current of Spirituality

experience in handling people and tricky situations? Am I quite sure that in order to be Christian I need no more than an enormous generosity and singlemindedness? In other words, do I depend on God's action or mine?

People get so used to doing ordinary things in an ordinary way without asking God to help them (on the mistaken assumption that they can address an envelope, start a car, brush their teeth, answer a telephone call on their own, without bothering to pray for supernatural assistance), that when it comes to important matters they tend to follow the same course. They forget that merely to pronounce the name of Jesus would, according to St. Paul, be impossible without the help of God. To make an important decision when in a state of doubt should prompt an explicit reference to divine providence. No amount of human wisdom can be substituted for the wisdom of God; no natural activity can bypass the action of God. It is God's world, and nothing in it can stir unless He gives it the power.

Once the action of God's providential will is grasped, as seen not only in personal affairs but also in the general ferment of the contemporary world and of its past history, surrender to divine wisdom becomes a lot easier. It is the reasonable thing. It makes any effort to force your own solution without the wisdom of divine providence unreasonable and positively lunatic. You plan a course of action which you are determined to pursue to the end, come what may. You have not prayed about it because you did not

The Current of Spirituality

think prayer necessary. You decided it was something which suited you, which you very much wanted to do, and that was that. Consciously or unconsciously you left God out, which does not mean the work is doomed to failure, or that sin was involved; it does mean that leaving God out is never wise.

It amounts to an insensitivity to the hidden movement of God's protective love, and hence a lack of spirituality, and that is why you sometimes find that having expended considerable labour in securing a desired objective you are dismally disappointed. You thought you had arranged for everything — and outwardly perhaps you had, but you failed to consider how you would feel when your ambition was gratified. You did not allow for the vital contingency which belongs to the dimension of the spirit and is consequently most subject to God's action. You could hardly be expected to know with any degree of certainty how you would react to the outcome (God does not suppose that you should) but you would have made a better use of your free will had you shown more detachment when you started. God always leaves men free, but the use of that freedom brings happier results when man does not try to force the issue on his own terms. There is nothing wrong with planning, nothing wrong with making every effort to realize your plans, but it is always better to plan within the framework of God's will.

The other side of the picture involves avoiding the mistakes which bring more trouble than you anticipated.

The Current of Spirituality

There can be no sure remedy for preventing you from making a fool of yourself, but in trying seriously to deepen your spirituality you are at least going about handling your affairs in the right way, whether outward or inward. Increasing awareness of God's protective love may not solve all your problems but it will tell you that your affairs are His affairs even before they are yours, and that problems which seem to you insoluble appear differently to the Mind which allowed them in the first place. It is a matter of absolutely believing God's love to be the answer to everything.

Admittedly, it seems a rather last-ditch argument to say, "God's love accounts for everything, but of course you are not expected to see it. God's will is the most important thing in the world but don't expect to know what it is." Spirituality is a process mostly conducted in the last ditch. It is a "looking not at the things that are seen, which are temporal, but at the things which are not seen, which are eternal." Although its activity is hidden (since it is the development of faith and rests upon what cannot be proved), spirituality is not so secret as to be unrecognizable: it is known by its effects, and the first effect of possessing a spiritual outlook is that you want God's will, even more than you want your own, whether or not you know what it is.

Without calling into question what the classic spiritual writers call "the mystical marriage" (used to denote the closest union of the soul to God), the parallel between the

The Current of Spirituality

divine and human relationship is worth noting. If each partner in a marriage considers the other's happiness to be more important than his or her own, the happiness of the marriage is virtually guaranteed. If one or other fails, the mutual happiness is endangered. The secret is to be unselfish by wanting the other's good. From the human point of view, the way to true spirituality is desiring God's will more than one's own. Very often, it is also the way of coming to know God's will: it is certainly the best way of disposing oneself to do it.

It is nothing new to suppose the phrase "God's will" can mean almost anything. It may be quoted as an excuse for doing your own will or for doing nothing at all. In the name of "God's will" people have practised, and accepted, every kind of injustice. "God's will" has been used to cloak the most secular enterprises. Many have hidden behind it a flagrant hypocrisy. The more religious people are the more "God's will" is bandied about. Therefore the necessity for a precise meaning of "the will of God."

Confusion arises from the assumption that "God's will" works the same as man's. The will of man changes day by day, hour by hour, according to his moods, his prospects, his passions, in response to the kind of propaganda he is exposed to, in response to the immediate provocation and opportunity. The will of God does not change. God *is* His will, His love, His wisdom, His power and truth. In human nature such qualities fluctuate but in God they are forever constant.

The Current of Spirituality

A most encouraging aspect is that God loves always and can never not love. He loves us not only when we obey but when we rebel, not only when we repent but when we refuse to repent. He loves us when we are in sin, even while we sin. That is not the sort of sentiment which a nice man feels for a poor misguided wretch. It is not because God thinks we are really children at heart and is willing to turn a blind eye, but rather because His love for us is an abiding reality. It is Himself.

It is therefore incorrect to speak of God "giving in" to our prayers, "being moved to compassion" towards us, "mercifully withdrawing His just punishments," and so forth. Our prayers do not change His mind, elicit His pity, or reverse a sentence. Then what do they accomplish? What is the point of praying? The value of praying for particular things may be seen as allowing God to put into operation something that He has willed all along. Our prayer has not changed His mind; the condition of its availability is that we should ask for it, so that He may grant something which from all eternity He has willed should be ours.

God's love continues even when man is rebelling against Him; but we must understand the distinction between loving the agent and loving the act. God can never love the sin itself, and He can never *not* love the sinner. God never wills a person to sin, nor does He ever not will a person to be free if he wants to. In His love He wills our freedom more than He could ever will our inescapable innocence. Our mistake is to imagine that God loves us with the same

The Current of Spirituality

kind of emotional love which gives us pleasure when we feel it towards our fellow human beings. God does not love us because we become attractive to Him or because He finds us responsive or agreeable; He loves us because He has made us according to a particular and unique expression of His will. In turn, He gives us the opportunity of loving back, and of returning to that love when we have withdrawn from it.

Spirituality, which is the development of the spiritual side of man in response to the influence of God, brings often obscure aspects of religion into focus. It does not pretend to clarify absolutely (its value would be nullified if it replaced the virtue of faith) but it does put into true perspective the mysteries and apparent inconsistencies of the religious assent. By cooperating with God's ever-present activity, spirituality can be developed to reveal not only the inward things of life, but the outward as well. Since human life is a mixture of the difficult and the easy, the incalculable and the predictable, the profound and the superficial, the pleasurable and the painful, the reasonable and the unreasonable, the just and the unjust — man needs an awareness of the life of the spirit of God if he is to avoid becoming dangerously involved in mere worldliness. He needs to be one with the unceasing current of the spirit of God.

3

Deeper Identification

The purpose of the Christian is (with St. Paul and according to the degree of his earnestness) "to know Christ and Him crucified." Yet, as we have seen, a man may live out his life as an undistinguished Christian without having to endure much more than an occasional criticism for holding certain religious views or for failing to live up to them. Relatively few are called upon to suffer as malefactors for Christ's sake, and fewer still to be stripped, scourged, and crucified. "With Christ I am nailed to the cross," says St. Paul, and again, "I bear about in my body the marks of Christ's passion." Can ordinary Christians like ourselves, in any real sense, claim the same?

Made members of Christ's body by virtue of our baptism, we do have a share in His passion whether we

The Current of Spirituality

volunteer for it or not, but that is not the issue here. Our object now is to examine what normally happens when one hands everything over to God and leaves it to Him to decide how much or how little of the passion He wants to see realized.

The individual considered here makes no conditions, asks only to be used, is ready to be exploited and is determined to accept without question whatever comes. So far, so good — it is the most promising disposition possible. The real thing, however, is not imagining heroic endurances and making a list of pleasures to be renounced; it is keeping quiet when God begins to take over. What God wants is consent to His operation. What follows is His work. The difficulty for us lies in seeing through the darkness which hides the knowledge of God and spiritual things. It is a kind of Gethsemane, wherein one is separated from all the securities and certainties which could previously be depended upon. The divine presence which could make all the difference seems to be no longer present and human companionship, even when it has managed to remain awake, affords no relief.

"The soul must be blinded and darkened," says St. John of the Cross in his *Ascent of Mount Carmel,* "according to that part which is related to God and spiritual things . . . and if he be not blinded as to this, and remains not in total darkness, he attains not to that which is taught by faith." No amount of argument or booklore avails. Prayer is the only worthwhile occupation, but one feels that there

Deeper Identification

has been a waste of time in the attempt to pray, and there is the suspicion that the relationship which once seemed so real is no longer within the realm of possibility.

What St. John of the Cross means is that beyond a certain stage your prayer is no longer something that you offer to God (gift-wrapped and candy-coated) but something which, without your knowing it, is coming to you in a quite different form and at a quite different level of consciousness. It is more an act of receiving than of giving, and as such, elicited positively by the initiative of God, is of a much purer order. You will not likely believe it to be true in your own case, but if you can examine it objectively (by-passing your own experience and evaluating it in the experience of another) you may see how the major obstacle to true prayer is self-sufficiency. The earnest Christian not only feels strong enough to discipline his own self-sufficiency but has enough confidence to overcome the difficulties of the life of prayer. Thus, if anything worthwhile is to come of his goodwill, the notion of personal spiritual competence must be reduced to nothing until only a sense of complete trust remains. How else than by receiving at God's hand the trials of ineptitude, frustration, and impotence?

Here, not merely by meditation but in a very real way, is an echo of our Lord's "My God, my God, why hast thou forsaken me?" There must also be an echo of the words which follow: "Father, into thy hands I commend my spirit." Without the further act of trust, the reproach of

The Current of Spirituality

being forsaken by God might be (in our case though not of course in the case of our Lord) a cry of self-pity and even of despair. Desperate perhaps, but not despairing; undergoing of necessity that desperation which comes of feeling suffocated by guilt, shame, and sin. In taking upon Himself the sins of the world, our Lord was not playing a role, pretending (for our sakes) to feel the anguish which we feel at the thought of our guilt, but was subjecting Himself to the same torment which we suffer and to an infinitely more agonizing degree. While we may not understand how someone who was sinless could endure the authentic experience of guilt, we should understand that if He had been going through only the motions of feeling guilt, He could not strictly be said to have entered into our shame and guilt. The act by which He freely chose to share our degradation would have been little more than a deceitful charade.

We must consider, therefore, both Christ's passion and man's witness to, and participation in, Christ's passion. Firstly, Christ's passion (allowing for the element of mystery which by definition is inexplicable) involves the conscious mind being temporarily cut off from God in such a manner as to envelop His whole being in a fog of fear, disgust, loneliness helplessness, and uncertainty. Allowed by the Father to remain in that state, it would have been no good quoting Jesus' own words to the disciples during the storm at sea: "Why do you doubt, O you of little faith?" Secondly, in the evolving spirituality which admits a man to a little bit of Christ's experience, an analogous process

Deeper Identification

takes place: awareness of life in God is obscured but, whereas in Christ's experience the life of God itself is deprived of its own knowledge, in man there is only a deprivation of the closeness of divine life, but those whose one desire is to live the life of Christ — approach the closest possible union with Him — find it a significant deprivation.

It must be promptly noted that the deprivation is the surest way to what is most desired. The paradox explains it. Enlightenment is achieved through darkness, and happiness is found through dread. In *Dark Night*, St. John of the Cross addresses the soul as follows: "When you see your desire obscured, your affections arid and constrained, and your faculties bereft of their capacity for any interior exercise, be not afflicted but rather consider it a great joy, since God is freeing you from yourself and taking the work from your hands." Those who would question the validity of that claim may find ample confirmation in the Psalms where the most often repeated theme is precisely the lament over the loss of God's presence, and following the dereliction is the joy of restoration. The whole of Christian spirituality can be seen in that sequence, put first in terms of human experience by the book of Job and then fulfilled in the gospels, of possession, deprivation, restoration. Without a Good Friday rooted deep in man's prayer life and extending to all the rest of his life, the joy of Easter is festal only and not factual.

4

An Unfortunate Side Effect

Spirituality without the essential elements of Christ's life, death, and resurrection leaves man using his faith as a culture and not as a religion. It is the error of the age in which we live that religion is resorted to for what can be got out of it by way of benefits, immediate returns, uplift and the like. "In it for kicks": an inelegant expression, but apt. Subjectivism and individualism are harmless enough in some respects, and they are needful in the psychological and social world; but where religion is concerned it is a cardinal error to espouse the esoteric. The man of prayer lays himself open to temptations which are more inward than those that side-track the politician, the business executive, the artist, and the engineer. Power politics, big business and the rest are vulnerable enough when it comes to investigation. Dishonesty and humbug are everywhere in the

The Current of Spirituality

world, and the Church is not without its particular brand of opportunism. If the world is sick so much more sick is the Christian Church which encourages contemplation without seeing to the safeguards of contemplation. Every age has its false mystics, and the present age has certainly produced its share.

In a real sense the critics of religion are right when they accuse us of idealistic dishonesty, attributing our psychological ills to an unwillingness to face the unpalatable facts of the human condition. We preach Christ and do not His works. We claim to see life through the eyes of Christ, yet turn away when we see what we do not like. Naturally, they argue, you are haunted with dread, fear, and shame; and are inevitably driven to psychotic breakdowns or to experimenting with escapes which do not satisfy. The solution (which our critics might claim is begging the question) is that true spirituality includes and involves dread, fear, shame and dereliction. If it is true spirituality and not a contrived contemplation, there will be just enough trust in God to prevent the soul from collapsing or taking refuge, say, in drugs. It is only a small margin, but an adequate one for God's purpose, and our own.

In the light of the foregoing it may be that the critics of religion have a valid case. In refuting the charges it is all the more important that the Christian should try to take to himself the whole life of Christ and not presume a piecemeal selection. Too often Christians pride themselves as representatives of the Christian ethic, but in the practical

An Unfortunate Side Effect

fulfillment of its implication they fall back upon a well-cushioned mediocrity. The more conscious they are of their inadequacy as Christians, the more vigorously they bluster about Christianity. Driven by self-loathing and despair they betray their eccentricity by drawing attention, not to Christ and his Gospel, but to themselves and their extreme views. It is not easy to live Christianity in our modern society. There are too many ways of getting around the Sermon on the Mount; there are too many ways of playing off one part against another. With its increasing respect for the subjective, the permissive society nurtures both mystic and mountebank. So much so that the subject himself (let alone those who form his public) is hard-put to know if he is truly a spiritual person or merely a show-off. If he gives himself the benefit of the doubt, he may fall to the evil of complacency; if he hates himself beyond a certain point, he dooms himself to further impotence.

Since the danger to spirituality of complacency is very real, a paragraph about it might be helpful. It is not a question of the smugness from which the ordinary churchgoer suffers from time to time; that is more readily exposed and the appropriate remedies applied. It is the problem of a false peace which prayerful people can build up, which is more menacing because of the spiritual safeguards which normally surround it. A good man, for example, a prayerful and charitable man, can render himself virtually immune from either the proddings of conscience or the admonitions of friends. By taking refuge in slogans to which he attaches his own meaning, by pious practices

The Current of Spirituality

which feed his own individuality, he claims a liberty of spirit which sets him apart. He makes no claim as such, to be in direct communication with God, but that is in fact what he means. He presumes to be his own master in an enterprise where it is vitally important that he should be seeking direction. All the ordinary expressions of religion serve only to bolster his personal infallibility. A life of extreme simplicity, fidelity to prayer, study of the Scriptures: he cannot be defaulted in any of these matters but on the contrary uses them with effect.

Before they have gone very far in the service of God most people find that the Scriptures can be used to support almost any theory, and that if one digs far enough historical precedent can be found for almost anything. On balance, it can be shown that the man who prays and disciplines himself is likely to be nearer the truth than the man who does neither. Surely the secret of steering a course among the hazards of the spiritual life is to pray constantly for humility. The truly humble man is open to direction, is not opinionated, always looks for the will of God, distrusts the pat formula, readily admits he may be wrong, and claims no invulnerability to delusion or errors in judgement. The truly humble man knows better than anybody else that he is never safe from the temptation, whether outward and gross, or inward and spiritual.

The misuse of spirituality can be as troublesome as the misuse of morality, which is perhaps one reason why people shy away from the life of prayer. They feel (quite

An Unfortunate Side Effect

correctly) that the more spiritual the good the more careful they must be in the handling of it; so they concentrate on immediate social and family responsibilities and avoid sticking their necks out into the unknown. The following will attempt to show how the denial of the spiritual side of human nature means the impoverishment of people as people, and therefore, the diminution of value in their work. That is not to claim that the materialist will be less effective than the saint; it is to maintain that the essential value of the work will depend upon the impulse which produced it. Elementary enough, but it supposes one very significant factor: not sitting down on the job.

Giving oneself up to God's will is one thing, taking the easy way out is another. Many who begin with the best of intentions find themselves in middle age, perhaps, persuaded that they can do no better than to let things take their course. The vision of what we have referred to as "destination" becomes blurred; the summons, under the heading of inspiration, is heard less clearly and inevitably the performance slackens. In the end there is little more to show for the project than a purely face-saving activity. It is this which brings religion into disrepute: the tendency on the part of religious people to cling to structures which they have allowed to become lifeless. Unfortunately the structures were designed for particular purposes which they may well have once served but somewhere along the line the vitality was allowed to grow weak. It is the prevailing temptation of every spiritual man to satisfy himself with a superficial spirituality which he justifies with a superficial

The Current of Spirituality

observance. The frame is there, but for all the good it does him he has dropped out of it.

Change the metaphor from frames, structures, and patterns to that of a body of water. A movie camera records the course of a stone thrown into a lake. The stone disappears, and concentric rings move out across the surface of the water. The illustration has been often used analogously to point one moral or another, but consider this variation: run the film backwards and what do you see? The ring of circles grows smaller and smaller until they reach the point of impact, and then the stone leaps out of the water into the air. The run-back might be used to show how people, particularly as they grow older, tend to close in upon themselves when at one time their movement was to expand. The touch of grace had struck the surface and penetrated to the depths; the mind broadened; charity spread out as far as was possible, knowing only the limits of opportunity. But then (though admittedly not at the pressing of a button or the turning of a spool) the process seems to go into reverse and the circles begin to shrink. Life appears as a series of incidents which go round and round, repeating the same mistakes and temptations and failures. One feels ringed about, increasingly confined to an ever narrowing area of containment. Psychologically and spiritually diminished, one no longer wants to extend himself or to risk bringing anything or anyone new within range. The only anticipation is that the ripples disappear and leave surface of the water smooth, unruffled and as lifeless as it was before.

An Unfortunate Side Effect

Such a situation represents a very real difficulty and affords a time of testing: whether or not to re-run the original "take" and guard against making the same mistake. What usually prevents it is the desire to preserve peace of mind and recollection, but is playing safe really inspired by a respect for the interior life or by the natural desire of the elderly and disillusioned to be left alone? Truly religious people should have allowed for disillusion and discouragement. Most people are disappointed in their hopes, but they need not make it an obstacle to their overall hope.

It is a curious fact that those who cite religious detachment as the reason for settling down within their own contracting circles are the very ones who crave affection and selective human relationships. They feel themselves to have shrivelled, to have been cutting themselves off more and more from social contacts; they become afraid of the loneliness which one part of them seems to cherish. They toy with the idea of making new circles again — wider ones — but they find it easier not to bother, and tell themselves there is no going back. This is their mistake. It is here that a return to the broader-based spirituality is the only alternative. Only thus can they truly find themselves again, psychologically as well as spiritually. Of course, they will still want the surrounding circumstances of life to be permanent and solid, the more so when they look back and see what they remember as an ordered way of living, but they must get accustomed to the idea of change. What was once thought to be stable and secure is now seen to be coming unstuck. Cherished standards, which in earlier days

The Current of Spirituality

were understood to be eternal (and so proclaimed by accepted authority), are cheerfully discarded by a younger generation. The knowledge that there is nothing in the world that can be done about it drives souls of the elder traditionalists deeper into solitude. Solitude is useful provided it is not a bitter solitude; then it is a wilderness of weeds.

There is, moreover, a tendency on the part of the older generation to remember their young lives as having been always more or less happy. How really happy were we when we were young? Are we deceiving ourselves? Having undergone so much mental and physical change are we capable of making any valid comparisons? Events followed one another then much as they follow one another now, but today we are bored by them whereas yesterday they excited us. So if the years have made us stale, it is our own fault and not life's or the world's. If the underlying psyche has not changed, we should be able to bring our attitudes into line with the ideals which we once held. Looking back over all the changes that have taken place in our lives it is natural to feel that even at the psychological level, strictly apart from the religious, we must have been better people when we were young. We were less suspicious of motives, we made friends readily because we took them at face value by what we judged to be a sound reckoning, we were ready to accept authority and did not question everything we were told; and above all we had hope. Precisely here, the spiritual enters and runs parallel to the psychological. The problems, as they arose, we met head on with an

An Unfortunate Side Effect

absolute confidence in God's ability somehow to show us the way. We met difficulties in prayer in the same fashion, not doubting for a moment but that God knew best if He seemed to leave us alone for a time. Our decisions were made in the light of His Spirit, or at least we hoped they were, because we did nothing without asking for His guidance. Perhaps the most abiding element of our service at that time was one of expectation: we had every interior assurance that we would somehow complete this life firmly united to Christ. Now, however, we seem incapable of completing anything; our prayer life does not bear examination; we jump from one decision to another, and always contradicting what we have previously decided to do; we look forward to nothing; we avoid meeting people; and we cannot bear to face the real self which is revealed to us when we pray.

If such a review sounds daunting it is only because we have not grasped the implications of faith and hope. The melancholy story of our trailing through the latter part of life with a broken wing (the main source of our dissatisfaction) is not the list of failures but a lacking of understanding of what faith and hope are really all about. God does not expect of the elderly the resilience of youth; He looks for acceptance and trust. At every stage of life and in every emergency, loving submission is the attitude required — even when reluctantly given. The fact that a particular virtue is the last thing one wants to practise takes nothing from the value of practising the virtue but rather adds to it. Faith and trust are not emotional reflexes but willed

The Current of Spirituality

responses. Either with pleasure on the one hand ("I always have a comforting sense of being looked after when I leave things in God's hands"), or with pain on the other ("I loathe all this but I suppose it must be God's will"), the soul makes the choice. It is the choice, the consent given deliberately in the highest part of the soul, that God wants.

So the question before all others in the matter of religion is, "Am I taking it on (or continuing in it) for the consolation (or credit, or security, or status) which it brings? Is it for my sake or for God's?" If you are honestly committed to the second of the propositions, the logic requires that you leave it to God's wisdom to decide what form your service is to take. If it is to be the way of faith and hope (charity will be considered later) then the more faith and hope you render to God the better, the more secret and unfelt the rendering the better, and you are among the privileged. All virtues have an outwardness and an inwardness, but in the matter of spirituality it is the inwardness of faith and hope that we most need to cultivate. Faith is more than believing doctrines to be true; hope is more than looking forward to eternal life in heaven. The inwardness of faith and the inwardness of hope should come to mean the same thing, the trust of one being indistinguishable from the trust of the other. Spirituality steers us to something comprehensive enough to be called either faith or hope; and the expression of it, and the power which keeps it in motion, is charity.

The subject of charity is necessarily approached differ-

An Unfortunate Side Effect

ently from that of faith and hope because of its twofold object, God and fellow men.† In relation to God the principle is the same as that of faith and hope. As faith is purified when we feel least like believing, and hope is purified when we feel least like hoping, so the love of God is purified when we feel least like loving. The normal way in which theological virtues are strengthened is by continuously exercising them when the emotional pull is all in the other direction. But when it comes to the love of neighbor, because of the personal element which calls the affective side of our nature into play, it is more than a simple matter of choosing. If fraternal Christian charity is to work properly, it requires as much warmth as we can muster. Charity demands that we love people for God's sake, but we must also love them for their own sakes. Regarding our fellow-human beings merely as occasions for the exercise of virtue is not what the gospel proclaims.

Visit an old folks home if you wish to see the difference between service rendered as a charitable duty and service performed out of love of old people. (The aged themselves are quick to note the distinction.) What people want is to be wanted, and you cannot make them feel wanted with only the intellect and will as motivators. The intellect provides the concept of charity, the will decides to

† *St. Bernard adds a third object of the Christian's charity, namely the Christian himself, but to go into this matter would make the present study more specialized than it sets out to be.*

The Current of Spirituality

express it, and from that moment onward the natural is as important as the supernatural. In the performance of every virtue the natural must be subservient to the supernatural, but in some virtues more than others the natural needs to be in greater evidence. Charity towards one's neighbor is such a virtue.

Charity (the subject will be dealt with more fully in the next chapter) is one of the virtues which is likely to contract if it does not expand, to die if it does not grow. Perhaps most of God's gifts to man are like that, designed to bring glory to the giver and happiness to the recipient, but when neglected they lead to trouble. Take again the illustration of the movie camera at work but change the subject photographed from a lake to a chicken emerging from an egg. The shell breaks, the chicken takes a few deep breaths, stumbles into the open and flutters what will soon be wings. Now reverse the scene and the bird re-enters into its shell. That can happen to our charity, and instead of new life we seek the old security of the shell. Either from fear or laziness or from having been repeatedly hurt, we stop beating our wings and think to be snug, safe, and stillborn. Not so much as a crack on the smooth, white, symmetrical surface to suggest that we were ever alive. In our shell we say, I am more at peace, I am not so vulnerable, and I am no burden to others. Charity, however, is meant to break outwards. At the risk of making endless mistakes, of having our love turned back to us, of having our motives misunderstood, our efforts ridiculed, we must persist in trying to extend our charity. We know it to

An Unfortunate Side Effect

be the fulfillment of the law, the bond of perfection, the quality which turns death into life, and which covers the multitude of sins — yet still we cling to the conviction that we can be happier, and perhaps even holier, by "not becoming involved".

5

What the Outcome Should Be

The touchstone of spirituality, as of everything else in the Christian life, is charity. Christians are not necessarily more consistent, hardworking, uncomplaining, detached from material things, or even humble and prayerful (though they have more reason to express these qualities than members of other religions) but they ought certainly to be the most kind. If we were to make a survey of those whose beliefs are other than Christian, or who admit of no belief at all, would our investigation find Christians heading the list in thoughtfulness, compassion, readiness to make allowances and to forgive? Too often one aspect of charity is exercised at the expense of the other. In our times it is the love of God in prayer that seems to be taking second place to the love of God in people. It is all the more needful, therefore, that the humanitarian side of charity operate

The Current of Spirituality

under the supervision of spirituality. Look to your love of God and, insofar as your love of God is not an exclusive and therefore a selfish emotion, your love of neighbor will surely follow.

In the examination of fraternal charity it is best to start at the bottom and work up. It is no good asking yourself if you can love, and lay down your life for, somebody who has done you nothing but harm and whom you dislike anyway, if you cannot welcome somebody who has kept you waiting or who has awakened you or who has interrupted a flow of thought. In his correspondence with his son, Lord Chesterfield made a great point of the need to be agreeable in every circumstance or provocation. In his view an affable manner, seriously cultivated, led to success. In our more competitive age success can elude the amiable, but there is a lot to be said, spiritually as well as socially, for making oneself agreeable. Not everyone is agreeable by nature, so it really is a matter of making oneself agreeable. Something which may begin with good manners, with being courteous because a social convention demands it, can become a charitable consideration for other people and in turn reveal an awareness of Christ present in His creatures. And with that must go supernatural compassion, supernatural desire to help, supernatural zeal for souls collectively as well as individually.

In such matters there is nothing like the practical test. When people play the game "What three people would you ask to have as companions on a desert island?", how often

What the Outcome Should Be

are you named among them? Are you one whom people would instinctively prefer to see rowing away towards the horizon in search of other shores? If Christianity is teaching us anything it should be teaching us to be easy to get on with. Again, is it to you that the lonely, sensitive, maladjusted or supposedly-ill-used instinctively turn in their distress? That says much about your Christian accessibility. If you are at all like many of us mediocre Christians, do you not assume an expression which discourages confidences and clearly indicates that you are the last person in the world to be safely asked for sympathy, an attitude which nearly shouts at the pitiful and pathetic to go away?

If Christian spirituality is to be something more than the devotional savoring of a dilettante experiment, it must be an open, straightforward, honest-to-God service. Right there, however, a problem presents itself: is there to be no limit to self-giving? One would like to think not but it must be admitted, however reluctantly, that in fact there is. The human being is capable of just so much, beyond which is the breaking point. The trouble is that so few know where the breaking point is, nor is it easy to know that limit in others. Most of us manipulate for safety and either evade the final challenge by escaping into one or other of a wide range of subterfuges and excuses, or else frankly admit that we can do no more.

Once more, spirituality shows us relatively how far we may go — and it is usually farther than we think. In works of charity the general rule is to stop short of any situation

The Current of Spirituality

which might positively contradict charity. To let your day become so crowded with good works as to leave you breathless and without peace-of-mind would be to go against the purpose of the good works. You can serve neither God nor man at any sort of supernatural level unless you allot yourself adequate time to pray. Silence and some measure of solitude are not luxuries but necessities. When you are quite alone and in prayer, you generate the energy to pursue your active works. Moreover, you must be able to depend on taking time to yourself rather than hoping to snatch it from harassing occupations. In His active ministry our Lord had little time to Himself during the day, but He went away at night and prayed.

For the Christian who wishes to live in the contemporary world in union with Christ there must be a planned resistance to nervous pressures. Tension will be inevitable and his willingness will be exploited, but when the danger signals appear he must slow down. It will call for firmness, detachment, and humility but unless he slows down, his mind will be in no condition for the prayer life. If his charity is to be worth anything, the prayer life must be secured to assure it.

In spite of the insistence (reiterated in every sermon and religious book) on charity as being the cardinal Christian value, we Christians do not measure up very well in comparison with other religious people whose values appear less specific. We are rightly put down by the living Hindu philosopher who notes that while we believe Christ to be

What the Outcome Should Be

God, we apparently do not believe man to be Christ. There is the humorous Islamic story about Allah and the creation. Having fashioned the universe, Allah, in the rapture of his successful work, decided to make a human being who was to be called a Christian. So he swept up what was left over of the mud and dust and made a man. The result so pleased him that with more mud and dust he made another Christian. After carefully observing the pair for a time Allah decided to make a third man whom he would call a Muslim, but the material he would use would be different: the blue of the sky, the sound of water rippling over stones, the sweetness of dates, the smell of fresh bread. The two Christians, what of them? Would they not be jealous of the third, and more magnificent creature? They would not have time to be (and here Allah chuckles into his beard) because they would be too busy quarrelling with each other.

For all our idealistic theory we Christians have from the beginning fallen far short of the teachings of our Lord; perhaps the higher the ideal the less capable we feel of living up to it, and so we come to see charity as a selective matter: having its label attached to one class of person and not to another, being signposted, mapped, catalogued and card-indexed, yet leaving large areas unexplored. One would think that experience of the spiritual life would lead us to a greater appreciation of its inwardness, and elicit a larger response to its more obvious call to human charity.

We know what St. Paul said about all of this to the

The Current of Spirituality

Romans: "Do not let your love be a pretense ... have a profound respect for one another ... keep on praying ... if any of the saints are in need you must share with them; and you should make hospitality your special care ... treat everyone with equal kindness; never be condescending but make real friends with the poor." To the Corinthians he wrote, "Love is always patient and kind ... it is never rude or selfish; it does not take offence and is not resentful ... is always ready to excuse, to trust, to hope, and to endure whatever comes."

It is not that in the world of today there is a lack of love, or that there might have been more of it in St. Paul's day: love is plentifully distributed in this century as it is in every century. Today it needs particularly, as it did in St. Paul's time, to be recalled from its self-serving expressions. It has to be seen in its supernatural context. No subject is more often talked about, written about, sung about in our secular society than love, and none so misunderstood. The emotion is what people make of it, and when the emotion stirred by one object has subsided they look for another which will arouse it again. Inevitably their capacity for love is either choked or jaded by desires which are mistaken for love. It is no easy thing for real love to come into its own when the approach to it has been diverted to the purely emotional.

Love means charity, and charity means God. As words, both "love" and "charity" have been debased: thus, when we read that "God is love, and he who dwells in love

What the Outcome Should Be

dwells in God and God in him", we wonder what it really means. The terms are different and seem not to apply to ordinary life when based on experience of ordinary love, and we wonder how God fits into the formula. "Love" and "charity" have always, in our language, been comprehensive terms. The more ancient languages provide a greater variety with more precise delineations. Even in English-speaking societies "love" need not mean only a particular kind of passion, and "charity" need not mean strictly a particular kind of benevolence.

God is love, God is charity. It is not that we must get back to the right understanding of words but that we must get back to the right understanding of God. God is not only the source of love but its end as well; He is its essence. When man fails to recognize the source, end, and essence of an object for what they really are, he will so misuse that object as to lose both his place in it and its place in him. Our understanding of the Christian life, even if we had never read the text "God is Love", should lead to the knowledge that the divine is the explanation of the human, and that unless we take a supernatural view of love we shall be left with a view which is not merely natural but animal.

It means that God, Himself undivided, asks of His creatures a love which has a twofold activity, and that each of these activities, having the same undivided origin, must either go to God or go wrong. Just as there are substances which have an identity of their own but which can be

59

The Current of Spirituality

chemically broken down into their component parts so that the parts neither relate to one another nor bear a resemblance to the whole, so the true and essential substance of love can be broken down in such a way as to cause a loss of identity all around. It is man, not God who separates love from charity and charity from love. Man must restore his fragmented concepts to their original unity. Without idealizing his love of God so as to make it unattainable or so humanizing his love of man as to restrict it to the notion of welfare work, the Christian has to pray his way towards God, who, being love Himself, will restore a more unified vision.

What does that mean in the practical terms of day-to-day fulfillment of the Christian obligation? First, it is better not to think of love as a Christian "obligation", because that would suggest something superimposed upon life, something which does not belong to the nature of life and which must be practised as a duty. More often than not a man may have to force himself to be kind, but he will discover that, compelled or not, his kindness will more nearly approach the ideal of charity when he thinks of it as service, and particularly as loving service. Charity toward man is the giving of the self; charity toward God is the giving of self; and that giving, whether seen as service to one's neighbor or as worship given to God, has both negative and positive aspects. There is the repudiation of one aspect of life, and the cultivation of another. It is the gospel paradox of having to die in order to live, of having to renounce everything if everything is to be enjoyed, of

What the Outcome Should Be

carrying the cross with Christ as the only valid initiation into the discipleship of joy.

It is the sacrificial side of love that is least appreciated today. What sort of love is it that burns hotly in the heart yet can not offer itself to be consumed on the pyre? As with faith and hope, love stretches out to something beyond itself in which immolation must be shared. Its symbols are the burning bush, the pelican, the phoenix, and best, because it was chosen by our Lord, the grain of wheat which can come to harvest only after its death.

6

Why Man Shrinks From It

People naturally shrink from anything that brings them face to face with themselves — which is exactly what the spiritual life does. Considerable honesty, not to say courage, may be needed if one is to face even the superficialities of life, but if one is obliged to take a good straight look at what lies under the surface, and particularly at what lies deep within oneself, one winces and runs a mile. Far greater honesty and courage is required to remain and face the facts. It is not that we are all born cowards, and that only the skillful craven can disguise it, but that in fallen man there is a natural antipathy to truth: there is both attraction and antagonism. He knows he is made for truth, that truth alone will answer his search, yet his one reaction, when presented with the stark truth, is to escape it. The evasive tactic never quite comes off but postpones

The Current of Spirituality

the day of reckoning. It is the contention of the present chapter that spirituality not only reveals to the soul the deeper realities and value of human existence, but also at the same time brings with it the strength to bear the confrontation.

Spirituality is not a dream, a trick of the imagination by which we can escape into unreality when life gets rough. Spirituality is a matter of the will far more than of the imagination. With God's help we can look at the everyday world and see the underlying realities; in fact that is precisely what man was created to do: to serve the Creator in a world of creatures.

Standing on the shore and looking at the sea you can think of the horizon as a meeting of the sky and sea in one of two ways. Either it is simply a line running right and left, and denoting the limit of your vision, or it is something beyond which other horizons lie which in their turn reveal other seas and lands and civilizations. The latter view has no part of fantasy. What your perspective tells you is provable fact. You may not be able to see beyond the line of the horizon, but your knowledge of the physical nature of the universe is adequate assurance of the facts and forms — that they do exist. If you wish to inspect them for yourself you may do so by travelling to them, but you do not need assurance of their existence. The line of the horizon is an arbitrary demarcation, a purely contingent affair, unlike the edge of a table or the drop of a shutter.

Why Man Shrinks From It

The acceptance of the world of the spirit can become a normal way of looking at life — matter-of-fact as looking at television, but with a new dimension added. Our knowledge of the spiritual nature of the universe should tell us that our physical horizon is not the only one, that the concreteness of things is not the entire reality, and that it is the added dimension of the spiritual which gives to the created order its total reality. So much for acquiring the habit of bi-focal vision. There is, in addition, something that appears to be a trap, but should be looked upon rather as a test.

You might think that the spiritual view of human affairs and the world in general would be a source of unmixed satisfaction, that at long last, apprehending reality in its most essential terms, you might relax. At last I have found security, you tell yourself; I need not worry; I can handle this transitory world and confidently anticipate the next; the real life lies beyond. Yes, but there is also a real life here; though its reality is relative, it is a living fact. Your new-found spiritual perspective means more responsibility, not less.

Experience would seem to prove that waking up to the world as it is (as it is in God's sight, for otherwise it would not be a real world at all), does not always change a person for the better. (This was what was intended by the above reference to a test.) As a child who encounters cruelty or lust for the first time can suffer a trauma lasting a lifetime, a soul can not only recoil from what is revealed in that more spiritually sensitive reaction but can actually take

65

The Current of Spirituality

refuge in his disgust. The danger is not worldliness, which is a straightforward temptation, but cynicism, intolerance, self-pity, superiority, inflexibility, and a refusal to understand the difficulties of others. Those unpleasant qualities lead to alienation where there should be compassion, self-absorption where there should be the desire to help, despair where there should be hope. Disillusionment is the worst possible inhibitor of the maturity which is the consequence of a greater spiritual sensitivity. Isolationism is the worst possible solution for contemporary man's great needs. The world today is starved for spiritual doctrine, and if spiritually-minded people hide away and refuse to preach and practice their ministry, the fault is theirs if worldly-minded people turn elsewhere for the satisfaction of their deepest hunger.

We Christians, particularly if we are between forty and sixty years old (after about sixty we tend to cease caring and want more to be left alone), are scandalized to hear of young people seeking answers to their psychological and spiritual problems in drink, sex, drugs, estoeric mysticism, or the latest fashionable guru. Are we blameless? We who are pledged to the truth, who are supposed in our prayer life to have glimpsed the truth, have been not altogether shining witnesses to the truth during the decades when the seeds of doubt were being sown. If our spiritual perceptions had been utilized more effectively, we might have helped the world in its groping pilgrimage and at the same time saved ourselves from disappointment, disenchantment, and the near despair of our present state.

Why Man Shrinks From It

The picture is in general outline; now examine the foreground details. The customary charge levelled at religious people is that of hypocrisy. With varying degrees of conviction and success, religious people slough it off, but since the object of these essays is to meet religious anomalies head on, storming the ramparts of complacency, a good subject for a beginning is evangelical poverty. In an affluent society, which shies away from such matters, it is particularly important that we think clearly about the Christian use of material goods. Who in our western civilization believes in the doctrine, and how many who believe in it live by it? It is of no moment now what an avowedly secular society thinks of it, but how Christians themselves should be thinking and acting. A society is as Christian or non-Christian as the individuals who comprise it. That brings us to the second point mentioned at the beginning, namely the effect of spirituality as a cultivator of frank, self-knowledge.

If he is serious in his undertaking, the man of prayer persists despite distractions, desolations, doubts, and the feeling of hopelessness. If he becomes so discouraged that he persists only in what is obligatory, giving merely token attention at that, he can hardly be called a man of prayer. The person we are speaking of is the one who cannot be daunted, but even for him more daunting than the difficulties which he recognizes and accepts as part of the Spiritual process, is the unvarnished sight of himself. Continuing prayer reveals it to him, and it is a real revelation. Seeing what the world tends to be like was bad enough;

The Current of Spirituality

even worse is the dismay which comes with the discovery of his share in it. Not merely the knowledge that the Christian Churches fail to live up to the evangelical counsels they profess, but the damning admission of his share of the responsibility for which he alone is culpable, is an unbearable sight. While he does not feel obliged to answer for the whole Church, or for the Christian religion, the Christian knows he must surely answer for himself. On present evidence he does not feel that he can.

For purposes of illustration let us assume our Christian to be one whose profession is religious and nothing more — a pastor of souls. If anyone is, he should be enlightened by spirituality, Christian values, evangelical counsels. He has heard the word of God and has preached it. What does it tell him about himself? One logical consequence of his prayer life should be an examination of his likeness to Christ in the matter of poverty. Poverty is the state proper to the apostle, the teacher and shepherd of souls. Poverty does not imply an exceptional vocation, something reserved for a particular sort of religious, but is the norm of life for any disciple of Christ. If there is truth in this, how is it that the pastor's main pre-occupation — even granting that the purpose looks primarily to the needs of the Parish — is the raising of money? The continual contact with large sums of money makes it very difficult indeed for a Christian to avoid the lure of luxury. He will understandably feel entitled to at least some benefits: the stereophonic record player, the colored television, a good car, the glass of sherry before dinner and the cigar to follow, the

Why Man Shrinks From It

golf-club membership, and the holiday abroad. What, though, has become of his prayer? Perhaps one day, in a moment of illumination, he sees himself as he really is. He is aghast, and hates himself, for he knows very well that what he sees is his real self; inconsistent, a parody of the Christian apostle, a hypocrite who has never lacked for reasonable and pious arguments to justify his way of life. Short of resigning his ministry and becoming an anchorite, for which he may feel no call and is probably too well established for anyway, there seems little enough that he can do about it; yet that little he must do or risk the further deterioration of his spirituality and ultimate collapse. The glimpse of his true self should at least convince him of the ease with which people like himself become the victims of affluent structures. When those structures are ecclesiastical they become (because there are so many altruistic explanations to support them) all the more difficult to escape.

The Christian layman, even if he is less "officially" committed than members of the clergy, also can re-examine his position. He can remind himself that Christ was not only born poor but chose to live among the poor; that He offered as His credentials the fact that He preached to the poor; that He congratulated the poor on their poverty and insisted that only by an exceptional favor from the Father could the rich find salvation; that He expected His disciples to make the explicity choice between two masters, God and money, and that (in the parable of Dives and Lazarus), it was not the cruelty of Lazarus that brought him down to

The Current of Spirituality

hell, but that wealth had blinded him to the real needs of others; that the young man would have joined the disciples had it not been for the great possessions that he could not bear to give up. The Christian disciple can also remind himself how the earliest disciples had to live on charity, that there were times when they were genuinely hungry, and that they were given no guarantee of present or future security. Such instances have not been cited simply to encourage the business man to review his use of the company car or his expense account, or whether his gambling debts can be offset by promising investments or the expectation of an inheritance. Each man has his own inventory of dishonesties, but it is the over-all dishonesty that is at issue here: the want of even minimal conformity to the pattern set by Christ. A man's prayer, whatever his status in the Church, should hold up to him a mirror of truth. Is there any likeness between what he sees and what he is meant to see?

St. James' analogy of the man seeing his own reflection in a glass and then going away and forgetting what he saw, forgetting his own face, is painfully relevant at every moment of our lives. It is never more to the point or more painful than when we have been offered the chance of redirecting our lives toward the image and likeness of Christ and have turned away to attend to other things. The spiritual life enables us from time to time to "look into the perfect law of liberty". What is revealed may be agonizing, but without such a clear revelation the process of purification and change can never obtain. Even before we know

Why Man Shrinks From It

what the light will reveal, we shrink, but so long as we do not refuse to look we are in the right way to *see*. It is only by closing our eyes, or by turning away to other things and refusing to turn back, that we disqualify ourselves.

Having opened our eyes and looked, the next move is to trust. Nothing need ever stand in the way of trust. We are not so poor as we should be and we are not so charitable either, we are not as resigned to suffering, not so eager to do the will of God as we should be; but if we can accept the humiliation of knowing ourselves for what we are, and are prepared to go on placing our whole confidence in God, we have made progress. If the first purpose of prayer is to give glory to God, surely the second one is to give us a knowledge of self — and not only that, but, as we have seen, a knowledge of the world and of truth. In fact it is difficult to see how any sort of reality can be arrived at by Christians except through prayer. Suffering teaches, love teaches, experience teaches, but what is taught by suffering, love, and experience can be fully learned only when seen through the larger perspective of prayer. In expecting prayer to accomplish so much for us, we are not looking for a short cut to knowledge or to God. Since prayer is faith there is no short cut. Still less are we trusting to ourselves praying: our whole trust is in the spirit which prays in us and through us. Our prayer is the prayer of Christ in us communicating Himself to the Father, in the process of which we learn, our spirituality deepens, and we come to see more of the truth.

7

Can It Change Its Course?

From what has just been said about Christ and not ourselves being the source of our prayer, it follows that the spiritual life does not change; the point is largely academic but it has its practical side. If we admit that Christ's action in the formation of our spirit of prayer is more important than any action which we can supply, the only conclusion we can draw is that the result, since it is His work, does not change from century to century. It is "Jesus Christ yesterday, today, and the same for ever."

Human nature's movement towards God remains substantially the same. Our mental attitudes, moral judgments and ideals differ from age to age and from generation to generation, but they are accidental changes: the variations are found in habits of thinking, not in thought itself; the

The Current of Spirituality

essential relationship does not move with the times.

That statement is not disproved by the psychological revolution which is taking place all round us, especially among the young: mass opinion in any decade or in any age group does not affect a principle, any more than mass hysteria on one occasion or in one city affects the nation. Spirituality is a much greater constant than nationality; it knows fewer divisions than class or color. The purist will avoid talking about schools of spirituality, because there is only one school: the Holy Spirit is the only teacher, and He does not change.

Since everybody's spiritual case-history is unique, the experience of spirituality will differ from person to person, but for the moment we are considering the objective and not the subjective aspect of the proposition. An individual's psyche may undergo modifications at different periods of his life, and we hear a lot about personality changes caused by environment or surgery or purely fortuitous happenings, but once in the current of spirituality the individual can count on the current following a certain course: while order may nowhere else be found, it is definitely found there.

If the individual man, or mankind as a whole, is to "reach full stature in Christ," there must be development. A human being matures physically, mentally, morally, aesthetically and, most important of all, spiritually. But he remains uniquely as God made him, and the laws which

Can It Change Its Course

govern his growth remain as God made them. The significant change in man's history took place when the human being became a new man in Christ; that, however, was an adoption, an incorporation, rather than an abrogation. God did not reverse His law; He transformed it. Man's life became so "divinized" that St. Paul could say "I live, now not I but Christ lives in me," which is what every Christian should be able to say. Without vainglory on one hand or vain humility on the other, he should be able to say, "I pray, now not I but Christ prays in me; I resist temptation, now not I but Christ resists it through me; I trust, now not I but Christ trusts for me." That insight comes with the current of spirituality, which cannot change, and Christians have been saying such things and depending on them since the beginning of Christianity.

The reason why the subject is brought up here, and why a case is made for a consistent tradition in spirituality, is that modern man is beginning to doubt the value of prayer and is wondering whether the time has come when prayer might be altered in some way to suit contemporary mentality, or perhaps dropped altogether. The argument is that, since modern man has no sure rationale for his existence, he has still less reason for the practice of prayer. The conclusion is that if spirituality has any validity at all, it is more in terms of the preternatural and the occult rather than in terms of Christian belief. If Christian spirituality were to come up with an answer to the problems of population explosion, atomic warfare, social justice, and human rights, modern man would give it a hearing. To him,

The Current of Spirituality

however, it seems that the Christian Churches have noticeably failed to provide those answers, and he infers that what was traditionally taken to be spirituality was in fact a mental condition adequately accounted for by modern psychiatry.

Obviously that line of thinking touches our concept of prayer and how it is to be expressed (or not expressed) by future generations of Christians. In an essay under the heading "Can Modern Man Pray?", a fairly recent issue of *Newsweek* (December 30, 1968) discusses the point and speculates on the relevance of prayer in the world of today. On the secularist stand, man no longer needs to pray. (Whether or not he can do it if he wants to is another question, and of secondary importance.) The author of the essay gives three reasons for which, in his opinion, the classic expressions of prayer must change: first, scientific discovery has made man able to manage without the help of God; secondly, what has been taught by the Church and the Scriptures lacks the kind of proof which is wanted today; thirdly, the basic assumption of prayer as being a personal relationship with God breaks down if there is no guarantee that there is a personal God to pray to. Put more briefly, modern man is without faith.

What brings the current objections particularly to people's notice is the ease with which they can be communicated. With the spread of television and radio, not to mention the increasing intimate coverage of the press, misgivings about every aspect of the Christian ethic are daily fare. The well-intentioned Christian who wants to know what our Lord taught, who is ready to serve Christ in the interior as well as in the exterior life, is at a loss. He finds a thousand answers (in an earlier age he would have been presented with perhaps one or two) which tell him that in looking for the interior life he is wasting his time. He concludes that there are no grounds for believing that there is an interior life; or, conceding that it is all right for those who have nothing to do better than cultivate their religious fancies, he chooses the "realities of life" which call upon all generous hearts for maximum humanitarian effort. Thus speak the media of the age.

We hear a lot about the crisis of prayer and the crisis which faces organized religion. It is not something new; we have always been faced with those crises. What is new is the fear which prayerful and traditional Christians feel about justifying the time they spend in prayer, while others are doing the work. "Your prayer life is a luxury," the activists tell them, "while what we are doing is a necessity." Contemplative Christians are at a loss to reply, and are afraid to bear witness to something which by its nature is hidden; the witness which is manifestly productive makes their kind of witness seem desperately insecure. Might it not be so much delusion?

Not only has the rapid advance in technology, sociology, psychology, and the human sciences made the activity of prayer seem too abstract for our materialistic age, but (and this is far more serious) it has made prayer seem

The Current of Spirituality

selfish. If prayer is to be allowed at all, the reasoning goes, it is to be a "realistic" prayer. That presumably means that it must be a prayer made in common (living witness) and of a kind that stirs the emotions enough to lead on to active works — uplifting and discernible returns. Such prayer has its place, but it is not what we are talking about when we discuss spirituality.

What the critics of the spiritual life do not seem to understand is that there is a difference between enthusiasm and dynamism. They look for a spiritual experience which will carry the soul into a busy world, where the influence will be seen to be effective. They do not understand a dynamism which works indirectly, and which is to be seen as a confrontation, not with people, but with God. By all means, a man's prayer life may overflow into marriage counselling, work for social justice, educating and preaching and serving, but if he is truly living a life of prayer he will know that it is the inward activity which affects the outward, and that even if there is nothing to show for it outwardly the inward must be preserved for its own sake, which in this instance means being preserved for God. It is because God's interests and the soul's coincide that the soul must not be afraid of worshipping in spirit and in truth, regardless of what that worship produces externally.

One of the phenomena characteristic of our age is the way in which humanistic activism suddenly manifests a yearning for retreat, mysticism, and the opportunity to be alone with the All. Such a yearning is not to be despised as just another search for sensation; often it is a genuine swing away from a materialistic culture, and represents a revolt against cramping social and economic patterns. The trouble is that it can itself become a culture and form patterns of its own. That would not matter if the cultists admitted an authority, a standard of validity. The whole point is that they are shaking themselves free of the old structures, of the establishment and of discipline. So inevitably they lack authenticity, and just as inevitably such spirituality as they are able to wrest from their experiments is subject to change. A variable spirituality is, as we have seen, a contradiction. A variable Holy Spirit is a contradiction.

It is a melancholy commentary on our Christian expression that there should be cultists at all. Their existence means only that those of us who are supposed to stand for authentic spirituality are not giving it to those who are searching for it and are willing to receive it.

If the interior life is set in the Incarnation-Death-Resurrection sequence, it does not admit of a process of selection. You cannot say, "I like the idea of being born anew, and the admonition that we have to rise above material cares to live in union with the Father, but I am leaving myself free to skip the intermediate bit." Whatever your devotional or Scriptural or liturgical attraction, whatever affinities you feel personally with the sacred humanity of Christ, you are aligned with a particular movement of the spirit. Your prayer as well as your baptism identifies you. If you pray, you cannot escape the logic of the

The Current of Spirituality

situation: as a cell in Christ's body you move as He moves, and in obedience to the orders which issue from His will and are communicated to His limbs. You cannot act independently of His members without rejecting the body and fashioning a new shape in your own image and likeness. The head must rule, and if the cells rebel against the head, they cease to draw their life from the body. The illustration of the body, worked out by St. Paul, is as telling as that of the vine and its branches which our Lord used on the last night which He spent with His apostles.

How about the good, honest, open-handed people who are never given to see life in relation to Christ? They are concerned about the state of the world, they help their neighbors whenever they can, they appear to be uncontaminated by the corruption which is on their doorstep. Is it just luck that they manage so well? Is it just by accident that we who worry constantly about the spiritual life manage so badly? In one form or another, that question is always being asked, but in the nature of the case it can never be satisfactorily answered. The Christian story — and this goes for spirituality, which is very much part of the Christian story — has to be told in terms of people; we are acting rightly, therefore, when we try to find out more about the soul's response to the challenge of the supernatural. Ideas are of greater interest now than perhaps they ever were (everybody is his own philosopher) but ideas cannot be known apart from the people who hold them. When it comes to the idea of a personal relationship with a personal God, we need to know all we can.

Can It Change Its Course

If the gospel is to be fulfilled, and if renewal and ecumenism are to mean anything, communication must occupy a vital place in the program. While the act of going out to others is of an importance equal to that of being open to what others have to offer, there is also the critical importance of the thing communicated. Communicate, by all means, but if you give only the impression which you want others to have of you — a pleasing image of yourself, when what is needed in exchange is a deeper understanding of truth — you would do well to drop out of the conversation and concentrate instead on living up to your desired image.

Genuine spirituality is naturally expansive. According to St. Thomas, the greatest spiritual gifts are forever straining to reproduce themselves. The contemplative soul moreover, is moved to share the fruits of his contemplation with others. You cannot have a spirituality *in vacuo* — an abstraction existing in a void — any more than you can have a true communication in isolation. Spiritual people need to be advised against excessive involvement on the one hand and irresponsible isolation on the other. The words "advised against" have been chosen with purpose, rather than "to choose between," because the individual person would find it difficult to make a value judgment and would tend to veer towards extremes, which would be difficult to put right later on.

Spirituality swings between the two most likely mistakes of fleeing and plunging. If it was disassociation,

The Current of Spirituality

uninvolvement, isolationism that once snared well-intentioned and prayerful Christians, the present danger is more likely to be the dissipation of spiritual energies in humanist enterprises, religious commitments, catechetical routines, ideological demonstrations and protest marches. Perhaps the best way to think of the demands which assail most zealous Christians is to bring in a distinction between two kinds of charity. One desires to stand before God in praise; the other calls for attention to a pressing need. The one represents a declared desire; the other an occasion which somehow interrupts the desire. In trying to solve the conflict, a man can scarcely err in choosing to serve God while bowing before the demands of his neighbor's need. He practices charity when kneeling silently, bearing witness to the glory of God; he practices charity when someone enters, switches on a light, and asks him to get the car and drive fifteen miles to meet a stranger arriving at the airport.

The second kind of charity, which mostly shows itself in communication, has at least the advantage of reducing preoccupation with the self. From the vast amount of nonsense that surrounds the subject of dialogue, confrontation, and participation, one fact emerges: self-centeredness completely vitiates communication. The person who is obsessively concerned with his soul-culture leaves no room for thought of others. He may be worrying about conscience, evolving a prayer of his own, avoiding sin, devising means to personal holiness, but if he does not relate his spirituality to similar processes which are going on in the lives of other people his individualism blocks the normal channels of charity. The more he keeps his spirituality to himself, the smaller and more lightweight it becomes; it can become a handful of feathers. There is a world of difference between the function of feathers in a pillow and feathers on a bird. If the life of prayer is to take wing, it must do so with others and for others.

Because the self is part of everything we do, we cannot expect to relate immediately to God or with others on a completely selfless basis. Even when we suppose we are being purposefully unselfish, we are in fact seeking fulfillment of the self in some measure. In the very act of trying to eliminate self, we have our own good in view: our "personhood" is seeking recognition. The right intention carries us far, but it does not carry us out of our selfhood. It is natural that selfhood, insinuating itself in a thousand secret ways, should inhibit the flow of human relationships. That process accounts for our inability to give ourselves fully to others or fully to receive them; but that very inability, instead of being a negative factor (still less a disqualifying one) can become a means of mutual understanding. It cannot lead to complete comprehension, because for mortals that is not possible, but it can lead to a greater sharing at a deeper level. A bridge affords a constructive analogy: it unites two separated points across what was hitherto a waste space. The bridge which has its foundations in humility (*humus,* earth) and functions according to compassion (*compassio,* I suffer with) is a positive factor in the communication exchange.

The Current of Spirituality

The only real breakdown in communication, whether with God or the Church or people, comes about when our selfhood, inevitably over-shadowing the negotiation, is allowed to have the last word. The approaches are now closed and can be opened again only when we have convinced ourselves that our dissident natures must not be allowed to get away with it. We are then enabled to start again from scratch, and we are better off because we are humbled to the dust, and God can begin to raise us up into what we are meant to be. (Dust is an appropriate material for fashioning creatures in His image and likeness.)

"Human relations" is an overworked term, yet it is a useful term if it reminds us that Christian relations must be human or they will fail in their purpose. Perhaps in trying to pursue the spiritual we pay too little attention to the human: God pays a lot of attention to the human, or He would not have become Man. If the human element in religion needs justification, the incarnation of Christ supplies it. Some religious people tend to equate human relations with social relations; they feel that in order to love God they must rise above associations which are mundane more than strictly spiritual, and thus they count it a virtue to dehumanize themselves. The effort to dehumanize either results in failure and induces a sense of guilt, or ends in success and makes for unreality; the mistake lies in thinking of the earthly and the spiritual as being in constant competition with one another: surely a better way of going about it would be to assume that a rightly orientated "mundane" life could prepare the way

Can It Change Its Course

for a better spiritual life. Since natural and supernatural are both aspects of the life that we lead on earth, and of the life that Christ led on earth, the more we can bring them into unity the better.

In being with God while we pray, we are in our proper element; in being with people while we mix and work and talk and laugh with them, we are equally in our proper element: deny life in either element, and we shrivel up. Take the homely illustration of the sponge (not the rubber imitation which, of course, is not a sponge at all, but the real thing that grows under water and is part fungus and, apparently, part animal). Removed from its native environment, the sponge shrinks into a hard little knot, desiccated and lifeless; put it back into water and at the slightest pressure you find it giving out what it absorbs, getting bigger while you watch. Spirituality is like that; communication is like that. The secret is to let them work together in their proper elements — elements which are not mutually exclusive, but, on the contrary, are common and mutually assisting. "Charity," St. Paul reminds us, is "the bond of perfection."

In every age of upheaval we can trace a widening of the gap between contemplation and action, between liturgy and labor, between study and imparting knowledge, between the spiritual and the corporal works of mercy. In the present-day setting, the emphasis is all on the second half of the great commandment, which has, for many people, taken the place of the first. Despite their talk about

The Current of Spirituality

community, Christians are losing their respect for unity: they should be closing the gaps, not extending them. They should see the great commandment as one, not as providing alternative options. They should understand that humanity and holiness do not represent different poles and purposes, but actually imply the same thing.

8

Communication

Unless the inwardness of Christian unity — the unity to be found in Christ — is appreciated, there seems little point in discussing ecumenism or human rights or equal opportunity for all. What matters is the human person, as he is in God's sight, and the programs which are promoted for the welfare of mankind, whatever the banner they fly, are of value only insofar as they assist the individual soul towards union with God. Once a program gets away from the personal human need of single unique beings, it might just as well be a scheme for beautifying urban sites. Perhaps the greatest need of our time is to get back the sense of the unit's place in the unity of the whole — and if we do not like to think of ourselves as units, we can at least think about the derivation of the word "unity."

The Current of Spirituality

Before ecumenism can become a reality, and if communication is to be of any help, there must be a recognition of what is shared in our common humanity: once that is grasped, and acted upon, sectarian barriers will fall. Until that aspect of basic spirituality and religion is recognized, every ecumenical gesture will be no more than a denominational maneuver which, unhappily, it very often is. Charity, however, covers a multitude of Christian bodies and we have the assurance that what all Christian groups have in common is the salvation of souls. Working outwards from that shared denominator, the Christian Churches may eventually justify Christ's claim that His Church should be one. Other marks it must show, by which searchers from outside may recognize its authenticity, but originally it was the Church's unity that verified it in the eyes of the world. "That they may be one," was Christ's prayer for the Church, "as you, Father, in me and I in you, that they also may be one in us: that the world may believe that you have sent me." Unity was to be the distinguishing note. How do our Christian Churches appear in the light of this?

But turn from the universal to the particular, and from Christ's prayer for the whole Church to His prayer for the group of individuals gathered round Him in the supper-room. "I pray for them; I pray not for the world but for them whom you have given me ... because they are yours ... and I am glorified in them ... Father, keep them in your name whom you have given me, that they may be one, as we also are." How do we, as individual Christians, show up in the light of that prayer? Christ went on to pray

Communication

that His followers should be sanctified in truth; He repeated the plea a moment later when he said that He was sanctifying himself "that they also may be sanctified in truth." So you get this interaction of unity, truth, sanctification: by being united, His disciples bear witness to truth, and in witnessing to truth they find their sanctification. Whichever way you hold the triangle, it stands upright on one or the other basic fact. It has to be a fact and not a mere wish because unity, truth, and sanctification are things for which Christ asked the Father, and as God Himself He could not have asked the Father in vain.

In case our investigation has taken us too far into implications, we might remind ourselves that the unifying force is divine love. A man's reason may tell him that racial discrimination is wrong, that war is an evil, that the death penalty needs a lot of special pleading if it is not a flat contradiction of 'thou shalt not kill', but he needs more than a method of deduction if he is to live his life according to Christian principles. He needs more than a universal benevolence towards mankind. He needs to acknowledge the Creator's presence in the created world, and to see in that presence the living dynamic of divine love. It is only because of God's loving presence in the world that a man can form ideas about justice, peace, and universal brotherhood. That he aspires at all towards a love that answers everything, and that must ultimately bring about the millenium, is simply because God manifests His care for mankind by establishing Himself in the midst of mankind and by being present in every human being.

The Current of Spirituality

As pointed out by Teilhard de Chardin in more than one place, the realization of God's love for man, and the response which man can give to it, can develop only out of man's disposition to recognize God's presence and action in the created order. Such a recognition cannot but result in the qualities discussed above: charity, truth, unity, sanctification. If that sounds too theoretical, we may have to be reminded that the process could not be more personal. "For the unity of persons as persons," says Teilhard de Chardin, "is a function of the direct relation of each to the one absolute, namely God, a relation that provides the ground of each person's dignity as an individual and, as shared, is the very basis of fellowship."

One may still ask exactly how practical the process is, from the point of view of getting on with people and keeping our minds on the thought of God in prayer. If it sounds impractical, it is because we attach too much importance to our own industry in achieving unity, in arriving at truth, in practising charity, in sanctifying our souls, and not enough to the action of grace. What we need is not so much to draw up a list of good resolutions about communication as to keep our minds and hearts open to the breathing of the Holy Spirit. If we were truly receptive, we would find our separate responses and concerns falling into place and assuming a unity.

9

Suffering

Spirituality has to allow for suffering, but it is not necessarily connected to it. Unlike what was discussed in the foregoing chapter, where communication was seen to be a necessary consequence of charity and truth, here it is a matter of two distinct entities which are designed to work in harmony but may very well not. There must be many sufferers who have no particular attraction towards the spiritual life; there are also people who lead spiritual lives but who seem to feel no particular desire for sacrifice. Spirituality and suffering are not interchangeable terms (to make them so would be to mistake both the character and immediate function of each) but it is safe to say that the spiritual man will not get away long without suffering.

All of that, however, is only a matter of opinion; but

The Current of Spirituality

what is certain is that the suffering endured by the spiritual man is different from that which the hedonist has to endure.

Lacking spirituality, human afflictions must appear as either punitive, arbitrary, vengeful, self-induced, imposed by blind fate or bad luck. It is only Christian faith, with its orientation towards Calvary, that can make sense of suffering. It is only prayer that can make it bearable, or even acceptable. When a man has learned through prayer that there is something that not even the greatest of sufferings can take from him, he can be at peace in the midst of disturbance. Like the supposed cell of silence in the heart of the tornado, there is an enclave within the soul which is proof against any distress one can mention. Apply the test. Think of what you fear most, and then see if there is any good reason why it should ever successfully invade the inmost recess of your being where you keep your trust in God. What does the religious man dread or hate? Giving in to his own weakness, losing his reason, standing by helpless while those whom he loves are being corrupted, seeing his life's work turned upside down and himself ridiculed, being deprived of the securities which Scripture and the liturgy and theology and the Church seemed to offer? None of those horrors need take God's presence from the soul: God still loves and can still be loved; and that love is always defended against the power of evil.

It is not what man is required to endure that deprives him of his peace of mind; it is his attitude towards his

Suffering

trials. The state of mind defines the suffering. Circumstances may be inevitable, but the suffering which circumstances engender is contingent, depending on what is made of it in one's own head. The material of life's sorrows and joys is provided; how we handle it is up to us. Some are endowed with a wisdom that teaches the secret of using circumstances to advantage, but, since most of us lack that wisdom, we do well to train our minds in prayer. Despite what is generally believed, prayer does not always direct us to take our sorrows lying down: it is much more likely to see the distinction between faith and fatalism. Whereas the fatalist adopts a supine attitude towards whatever goes wrong in his life (more often indulging in self-pity than offering his trials to God), the Christian whose prayer is leading him deeper into faith shows a robust reaction. Putting his trust in God, he fights the evil which oppresses him, especially if it is an obvious one like cruelty or calumny or injustice, and only when he is quite sure that God means him to suffer the consequences of the evil does he resign himself in a spirit of detachment. His resignation at that point is an act of humility and dependence; resignation at the beginning might have been an act of laziness. Quietism can be more harmful to religion than venturing risks: to sit with folded hands and await the worst is no part of the Gospel of Jesus Christ.

Most people might agree that at the top of the list of trials to which our human nature is subject, whether we are considering the Christian or anyone else, is fear. In one form or another, all of us experience that crippling emo-

The Current of Spirituality

tion: the fear of sticking one's neck out, of going against advice, of being conspicuous, of starting something which one may not be able to follow through or control when it has been followed through. People, sometimes because of a mistaken spirituality, take the line of least resistance and yield to such fears. So, of course, inertia results. "The kingdom of Heaven suffers violence and only the violent bear it away." The timid man lets it slip between his fingers. The worthwhile things must be taken by storm, and that means assuming responsibility and often considerable risk. Prayer gives one the confidence to do that and lets one know what risks may be taken and when. This is not to claim that prayer favors the foolhardy, or that the waters of the Red Sea will part in return for a few elevations of the spirit to the Lord. The claim is only that the timid will be given to see the folly of their timidity, and consequently will be able to move on to a greater trust in God.

Fear can often be mistaken for the diffidence which can be a sign of humility; but it is like any other weakness and should be firmly mortified. Here, however, we shall consider fear not as a weakness but as a trial. It is not only the straightforward fears that we have to buttress ourselves against (fear of being run over, of being trapped in a fire, of becoming a helpless invalid, of being beaten up by thugs) but also fears that are really not fears, though they inhibit us and lessen our ability to serve either God or man. Such fears include unwillingness to meet people, the desire to keep on the move to avoid a settled form of work,

Suffering

wondering if one shall be able to sleep, if one is well enough to get through the day's demands, hoping one's appointments will be cancelled, expecting the telephone to ring, knowing the day will come when one cannot remember a prepared speech, when one will find oneself locked in a bathroom, will lose one's keys or address book or passport. With every fear there is an accompanying warning against further effort and the temptation to escape that fear. More than any other temptation, excepting that to suicide (which is itself the desire to escape from what is feared) the slow quiet hard-to-identify temptation to fear robs a man of his sense of purpose. Everything conspires to make him afraid of trying to overcome his fears. Taking the line of least resistance can cramp, if not stifle, the soul's faith, hope and charity: nothing grows faster than the feeling of inferiority, and it is fed by every new withdrawal. From the belief that he is good only for bumpkin occupations, a man can go on to lose his self-respect, his confidence in God, his sense of fellowship with others, without which man is nothing.

Psychologists tell us that *angst* (the feeling of deep anxiety just described) is a characteristic feature of our society, and that it accounts for the loneliness, indecision, sense of guilt, disillusion and escapism which we come across every day and which leads to social as well as psychological disorders. Conceding their findings to be accurate, we must yet hold out the Christian remedy of the Gospel, particularly that set forth in the Sermon on the Mount. It is not as though *angst* had come upon the world

The Current of Spirituality

unforeseen by God; indeed, as in the case of every other cross, Christ is at hand to help us with it. The doctrine of "be not solicitous" which runs as a refrain through the sixth chapter of St. Matthew is an exhortation that must apply in every age. The Sermon on the Mount was addressed not to the successful people, the thrusters, but to anxious, nervous souls who were constantly worrying about themselves and their future, and it has been addressed to the same sort of people ever since. The doctrine that "perfect love casts out fear" is addressed not so much to perfect lovers, who can be assumed to have knowledge of it already through experience, but more to hesitant and timorous souls.

Our Lord preached trust, love, and prayer as remedies against man's natural nervousness. The disciples in the boat were told that they would have nothing to be afraid of if only they had more faith, and they were reassured on that point when Christ said that not even a hostile world nor "the prince of this world" himself need alarm them "for I have overcome the world." It is worth noting that even before this, God's angels were already spreading the same message. Reading St. Luke, one would think it must be the special work of angels to go about persuading people not to be afraid. "Fear not, Zachary, for your prayer is heard . . . fear not, Mary, for you have found grace with God." Turning to St. Matthew, we have an angel telling Joseph not to be afraid, that Mary his wife had conceived of the Holy Ghost. Back to St. Luke again, and we have an angel telling the shepherds on Christmas morning: "Fear not; I

96

Suffering

bring you tidings of great joy." It appears that *angst* is not peculiar to the twentieth century; but even if it were, we would have the answer to it in the example of our Lord, whose fear in the Garden of Gethsemane surpassed any fear that man has experienced before or since.

Fear is not the only obstacle to be encountered on the way to God. Trials which have no particular relationship to fear include such ordeals as depression, boredom, overwork, exhaustion, breakdowns, vocational upsets, homesickness, misunderstandings, broken friendships and wasted opportunities. Though such sufferings may be brought on by ourselves, we are helped to endure them by the amount of prayer that is applied to them. It would be a mistake, however, to imagine that, in order to obtain God's help, we must spend our prayer time on the particular suffering of the moment, asking for the grace to meet it. To do more than refer the matter briefly and in general terms to God would only clutter up our prayer with moans and mournful appeals. Under pressure of suffering, our prayer should remain as far as possible what it always is; suffering should deepen our prayer, not distract it. While the immediate occasion of the suffering (in the time of temptation or during any other emergency) should call for immediate recourse to prayer, it is the overall spirituality, the effort to be recollected, which proves the main support when things go wrong.

Sin excepted, nothing is outside spirituality's sphere; yet, in the sense that people who are trying to lead the

The Current of Spirituality

spiritual life more readily repent, even sin comes within its range. Certainly spiritual people see sin more clearly for what it is, and are more conscious of it in themselves and others. Where the sin of others is concerned, this consciousness leads to compassion.

So much for the spiritual life and sin, but what about the spiritual life and temptation? The answer comes from the Epistle of St. James: "Count it for joy when you fall into divers temptations." That surprising statement does not reflect everybody's experience, but since it is inspired by the Holy Spirit its truth bears examination. St. James goes on to explain how "the testing of your faith produces steadfastness." That is the point of temptation: it acts as a blow torch, burning and cleansing at the same time, and, as in the case of sin, produces from one's own weakness an understanding of the weakness of others. So long as we turn to God when tempted, we have nothing to fear, but on the contrary much to be thankful for. Faith and humility are being fire-tried, compassion is coming down out of the skies and assuming a new meaning. St. Paul's doctrine about virtue being made perfect in infirmity brings consolation at the level of real life. We must experience our weakness, not merely give a nod to the proposition, if we are to be educated in strength — but the process is painful, and we have to reckon with it.

Finally, the spiritual life teaches us how to control our outward reaction to suffering. By it we learn not to expose more of our emotional response than is necessary. For

Suffering

religious people, no less than for others, there is always the temptation to play the martyr. So much of life consists in disguising our feelings one way or another that it would be sad if we could not keep to ourselves the secret, though uncomfortable, gifts of God.

10

Happiness

Everybody is concerned about happiness — not only his own, but that of others: happiness generally. As Christians we should take literally the text which we hear often but seldom listen to, "Seek ye first the kingdom of God and His justice, and all these things shall be added to you." Truth often appears trite.

One thing which the spiritual life teaches is to give greater attention to the durable qualities and less to the exciting ones. Contentment sounds dull to somebody who is looking for ecstacies of delight, but contentment can be made to last, while ecstacies tend to fade. Holy people have their joys but they do not rest in them; joys are accepted with thanksgiving but also with detachment. Pleasure is not allowed to become a greed. With most of us, greed is one

The Current of Spirituality

of the major incentives, which means that when frustrated we find it hard to bear our disappointment gracefully. It would be easier if greed did not survive the disappointment, but it does. In the case of truly prayerful people the problem does not come up; they have learned to curb both longing and disappointment. They have put things in their proper place and can see beyond them towards God and the things that really matter.

We can put ourselves to the test. Do I meet the unfulfillment of my hopes (the term can cover plans, ambitions, worldly undertakings, on one hand, and, on the other, religious enterprises and spiritual aspirations) with calmness or bitter resentment? When I have failed, but another person has succeeded, am I ready to try again (if I believe God wants me to), or do I sulk and give up? Does a failure leave me in a state of peace with a greater desire for prayer, or does it make me restless, ready to take advantage of my exhaustion, less disposed to offer myself for God's work in the future — if that is the way He is going to treat me? It is told of the Roman ruler Antoninus Pius that as he lay dying at Lorium in Etruria he was asked by one of his friends to sum up in a few words the philosophy of his life. A single word was enough; the answer was, "Equanimity."

It is not that the spiritual life demands the choice of equanimity over happiness, but rather that each is the sign of the other. That is the serenity which we associate with sanctity. One feels when one is fortunate enough to meet a

Happiness

saintly person that the warmth of his charity does not come from a crackling fire, blazing away for the comfort of all, but from a calm steady glow. When our Lord speaks of leaving His peace to His disciples — a peace different from any that the world offers — He is talking about a quality which may or may not be "happy" in the accepted sense. A few hours after giving that peace which was His alone to give, He went to Calvary. "These things I have spoken to you so that my joy may be in you, and your joy may be filled." He expressed serenity even in the expectation of extreme suffering; that serenity was something which our Lord surely radiated throughout His life. That is how we should think about Christian happiness: it is inward, it comes from the Father and the Holy Spirit, and it communicates itself to others.

If one changes the metaphor from a fire to a pylon, a tall metal structure that carries electrical current, one gets a clearer idea of the act of transmission. (Originally the word "pylon" meant a gateway, and came to be given to the towers which flanked the gateway.) People can be thought of as pylons, and it is a Christian duty to be one. Human beings must, of course, retain their own identity, remaining separate from one another; but as the pylon once formed the entrance to the temple, sharing the same weight and bearing witness to what lies deeper within the building, so the Christian does the same. As the modern pylon transmits to other pylons down the line a force which is not of its making but which is for the good of the world, so the Christian passes on the grace he has received. One such

The Current of Spirituality

grace is tranquility, peace, serenity; or, if you prefer, happiness.

Nobody, however, not even a saint, can put peace, happiness and the like into another. If each person made it his business to make other people's happiness more important than his own, obviously the world would be a happier and more peaceful place than it is; but man, who cannot make himself responsible for his own happiness, can hardly make himself responsible for the happiness of his fellows. God alone is responsible for planting human happiness. That is why we should acquire, by our prayer life especially, the same view of happiness as God's. That is why we must think of it as Christ's prerogative — *"my* peace I give to you." A man gets nearest to it by accepting the life that God gives him, but no amount of accepting will necessarily guarantee enjoyment. Enjoyment, though he may confidently expect to have it at least occasionally, is still a gift. There is something rather sad about a man *trying* to enjoy himself, but there is nothing sad about a man who finds peace when enjoyment has been denied him. He is always given grace for it, but he does not always accept that grace. It is only the exceptionally generous man who can accept the deprivation of enjoyment gracefully.

It is a curious and significant fact that since pre-Christian times the Cup has been the symbol for two elements of life which run contrary to other another: pleasure and pain. When we recall Calvary, that should not surprise us: what we think of as the Chalice of Salvation

Happiness

must contain vinegar as well as wine. If vinegar is only a kind of wine gone wrong, sorrow is nearly always a kind of happiness in reverse. An inference to be derived is that our understanding of happiness and sorrow depends not upon the exclusion of one or the other, but upon the experience of both, seeing the one in the light of the other. Literature, classical and modern, spreads itself about equally on the two subjects, the difference in the treatment commonly being to pose questions as to the nature of happiness while accounting for the reality of suffering.

Christian and non-Christian writers agree that pain and pleasure exist in the mind rather than in the senses. That is a matter not of theology, but of philosophy, psychology and common experience. Scholars of every civilization — Indian, Chinese, Hebrew, Greek, Roman — have sought by probing into the thoughts of man and even into his dreams to prepare people for suffering. They have also tried to show people where to look for happiness. In every culture worthy of the name, however, the soul is taken to be the seat of experience. "Men are not worried by things" wrote Epictetus, "but by their ideas about things. When we meet with difficulties and become anxious, let us not blame others but rather ourselves: our trouble lies in our ideas about things." Greek philosophy brings us thus far, but Christian philosophy takes us the rest of the way. We look up from the shadow to appreciate the substance. We see the shadow of the Cross, true; but we look up to Him who hangs upon the Cross. "I preach Christ crucified," says St. Paul; not Christ downcast, but Christ crucified — uplifted.

The Current of Spirituality

"I, if I be lifted up, will draw all things to myself." The New Testament works outwards from the crucifixion of Christ, drawing all men to Him and then sending them out again to imitate and bear witness to Him. Through Christ's crucifixion and theirs — theirs a mere token by comparison, but painful enough in the enduring — His followers come to share in the triumph of the resurrected Christ. That is true Christian happiness, anticipated by faith during this life and to be fully enjoyed only in the next.

The Cross and peace function, as we have seen, not by turns, but together. Certainly St. Paul saw no contradiction, "God forbid that I should rejoice except in the cross of our Lord Jesus Christ." "Peace be to you," said our Lord to His disciples after the resurrection, "and He showed them His hands and His feet." The capacity to see how the whole of Christ's doctrine, and the whole of our religious response, can come together into unity is a grace which flows from a deepening of the spiritual life. Without prayer to give that perspective, we view the lessons of our faith under separate headings; our obligations as Christians impose themselves as the occasion arises, and our worship is fragmented. Relationships with people and with the world become piecemeal affairs, regulated by circumstances. In the perspective of prayer, however, the soul sees not only a pattern of God's ordering of the universe, but a focus which includes everything. The appreciation of oneness — not merely harmony, but unity — is something which shows itself again and again. Dante says at the end of *Il Paradiso:*

Happiness

> Fixing my gaze upon eternal light
> I saw enclosed within its depth
> Bound up with love together in one volume
> The scattered leaves of all the universe:
> Substance and accidents, and their relations
> Together fused in such a way
> That what I speak of is one simple flame.

At a less exalted level, it is worth noting that many good religious people imagine themselves to be miserable because they are not so happy as they were when they were younger. The mistake is to compare one's present state with what one remembers of another. For one thing memory plays tricks, painting sunlit lawns and cloudless skies, and for another it is easy to confuse happiness with high spirits. If looking into the future and dreading possible calamities is an absurdity, it is no less asking for trouble to look into the past and rake up lost raptures. "There is no sadness," wrote T. S. Eliot, "like a joy remembered." It also works the other way; there are few satisfactions like knowing one has come through a period of wretchedness. The secret of it, and one which a man should study as he grows older, is to be able to say with St. Paul: "I have learned in whatsoever state I am to be content therewith."

It would be foolish for young people to count on being able to keep up indefinitely their zest for life; but, of course, young people do not think like that: they take life for granted. It is only when people have left their youth behind that they start pining for the spirit of it; what is

The Current of Spirituality

thought of as happiness is really no more than a lot of pleasant associations. The error is not a new one. "Oh that I were in the times past," sighed Job, "as in the days when God watched over me; when His lamp shone over my head and I walked by his light in the darkness ... when the friendship of God was upon my tent, when the Almighty was yet with me." It was his memories, not his afflictions, that unsettled him. What Job needed to learn, and in fact did learn eventually, was that the gifts of God, whether material or domestic or spiritual, were not to be appropriated but held in fealty. Once a man starts hoarding the things that God has lent him for his use, he is no longer a steward but a self-appointed proprietor, and happiness is one of the things he had better not try to hoard or he will find it slipping away from him.

The holy man Job was pursuing a much safer line of thought when he proclaimed boldly: "The Lord gave, and the Lord has taken away; blessed be the name of the Lord ... naked came I from my mother's womb, and naked shall I return." The natural law so plots the curve of living things that they reach their peak of excellence and then decline. Fruit ripens and then rots, milk after a time turns sour, man develops physically and intellectually until he can develop no more and must be content to grow old. As men grow older, many of them resent the lessening of their energy, of their ability to influence young people and to hold the attention of their contemporaries. They don't like to admit that they cannot remember names, cannot laugh at people's jokes, cannot follow an argument, cannot

Happiness

express their ideas (if any) coherently, cannot see or hear or move about as they used to do. The point is that if they look back now, they will spoil their chances of finding the happiness appropriate to their particular stage in life. If, on the other hand, they can say with Job, and without self-pity, "the Lord gave, and the Lord has taken away; blessed be the name of the Lord," they will enjoy a satisfaction unthought of twenty years earlier. It will be a quieter kind of happiness, but in many ways a more reliable one: it will not be so much at the mercy of impulsive decision, romantic hazard, or cut-throat competition.

If a spiritual outlook is needed when human faculties are failing, it is all the more in demand when the powers of the soul seem to be declining, for therein is found the real test, possibly the final test, of faith. The lives of holy people seem to reveal a fairly consistent drift of thought; the Job syndrome, in purely interior terms, is being reproduced. The individual feels himself to be losing his grip, to be looking wistfully back to a stage in his spiritual life when God meant more to him — when he had an anchor, direction and hope. Added to that sense of spiritual diminishment (the sense of having lost the one thing, namely God's presence, which would have given him security), he becomes increasingly aware of the image that he is creating in the eyes of his one time followers. He can no longer command, and justifiably so in his own opinion, the confidence of others. Not unnaturally, it causes him acute distress to know that people whom he had hoped to lead

The Current of Spirituality

to God are disappointed in his leadership and are seeking direction elsewhere. The story is reproducing itself: "the Lord gave, the Lord is taking away." What can he do now? There is but one answer. "I have learned in whatsoever state I am to be content therewith." That is faith, that is hope, that is (though the one concerned does not appreciate it as such) charity.

11

Failure

Spirituality has standards of its own by which failure and success may be measured. The whole thing turns on how the outcome of any undertaking is seen by God. More often than not we are in no position to see what God sees, to know what God knows, but one thing is certain: we cannot go wrong by refusing to evaluate an act of faith by our own human standards. In life as we ordinarily know it there is no necessary justification for failure, but failure there is, and it must be allowed for even by the successful and the worldly; but without a setting to give it value, failure can be seen only as a drawback — or at best as a salutary discipline in the formation of character. It is said of Diogenes that he interrupted his lecture on one occasion to address a statue and ask it to lend him some money. His students, puzzled by what appeared to be a mental lapse,

The Current of Spirituality

showed a proper solicitude. "I am schooling myself," explained the philosopher, "to disappointment." Lessons in detachment apart, a materialistic and highly competitive society can hardly be expected to see advantages in failure.

In its Gospel context, failure takes on an altogether new meaning. Each successive personal failure should bring us a step closer to the failure of Calvary, and so to the success of the Resurrection. Every human failure can be seen as an envoy from God, a herald: instead of having a debilitating effect (as it must in the case of people who have only the outward to go upon), failure can enliven our awareness of God and stimulate our spiritual reactions to the affairs of life. Where the materialist rationalizes his failures, makes excuses for them, and lays the blame on any number of things, the man of prayer pushes his failures upwards from resignation to acceptance, from acceptance to thanksgiving. The last is the ideal to be aimed at.

There is always the danger of making a cult of failure. For some people failure can become a status symbol; ruins and wrecks hold a special fascination, and the desire to appear forever broken on the wheel of fate is simply another form of exhibitionism. At the time of his trial, Oscar Wilde seems to have cherished the role of sublime victim, and still more clear is the hugging of defeat in the last hidden years of T. E. Lawrence. It has been suggested that General Gordon, a deeply religious man but given to the theatrical, cast himself in the dying-god part and that he need not have been killed at all. Be that as it may,

Failure

spirituality, since it takes its stand on the truth, should steer people away from the dramatic and not lead them into it: the plaintive wail and the wringing of hands have nothing to do with a good Christian failure.

It must be admitted, however, that there are those who, without suffering in the least from the failure-wish, seem to go through life cheated of merited rewards. They have only to attach themselves to an enterprise and at once it begins to crack. Their jobs, investments and marriage go wrong, and on the day when at last they set their feet on the road to certain success a car runs into them. (The failure-prone are not necessarily the weaklings of society; the strong are equally liable.) What those people must seek is a mixture of natural resilience and religious faith. They should be like those toy figures standing upright on a curved and weighted base: every time they are slapped down they bounce back to their upright position: there is no law that knocks them over, but there is a law that pulls them up. Man is not governed by a law of fate that predetermines his failures; but in a fallen world, failure has its place, and because of the way the world was redeemed that place has become an honored one. Not everybody, of course, is going to believe that statement: only a spiritual view of life will take account of it.

Failure, like every other kind of suffering, is meant to evoke a feeling for others who are being treated to the same discipline. If failure cuts a man off from others who have failed, it evokes only self-pity. The moment it be-

The Current of Spirituality

comes an indulgence, a luxury, it not only ceases to have any spiritual value but becomes a pathetic hindrance; it invites ridicule instead of help from others. It is a sad paradox that without compassion, the pathetic can be made to look absurd. Even in the exchange of sympathy, however, much is to be avoided. There is an unfortunate magnetism about failure that brings people together so that they may wallow in their failures together. To wallow in failure with others who have failed is even worse than to wallow in one's own failure. Wallowing in anything is to be avoided, whether in failure or success, in possessions or popularity. The man who sets his sights on spiritual things and who is beset by failure had best not take himself and his failures too seriously, but rather take seriously the matter of faith and hope. Once again it is "I have learned in whatsoever state I am to be content therewith."

Thus far our discussion has had to do with failure in outward things. It is in the inward sphere that we need a greater resilience and a greater fund of faith and hope. "No man is mature," Senator Ashurst said, "until he has tasted sorrow and humiliation: defeat at the summit." The summit, as far as we are concerned, is the spiritual one, so we must know what to expect or the peak will seem even farther out of reach. Spiritual maturity is the ability to keep on climbing even when we appear to be stuck, even when we feel that we are slipping back. (That, as will be stressed in a minute, refers especially to the climb of prayer.) Maturity is not immunity: the thoroughly spiritual man is not impervious to the upsets and the collapses

Failure

which come his way — he feels them, but he rises above them, and in that sense governs rather than is governed by them.

The feeling of failure presses deepest (and the more spiritual the man is the more he feels it) when one judges that he has failed not only himself and others but God. Take the case of someone who starts off by way of stages outlined for him in books, with every expectation of mounting to final union with God. According to the classic form, he offers his body, heart, and soul for service. Then comes the conviction that nothing has happened and that nothing is going to happen; he wonders whether anything was ever meant to happen, and whether the impulse towards spirituality did not come from self in the first place and not from God at all: everything points towards that conclusion. The heart which he had thought could be trained so exclusively upon God now resists an undivided direction and tends to express itself more humanly. He had confidently believed that he would be occupied in devotion for the rest of his life, but now he is left barren, arid, and groping. Bereft of an earlier enthusiasm for prayer, the soul hits upon the idea of seeking more solitude as a means of compensation: solitude, however, does not bring the presence of God; it brings loneliness and restlessness. Acts of trust are, of course, made in prayer but often they seem to be nothing more than words; books and sermons are of little help, even retreats seem to hinder rather than help. The tension confirms the melancholy conclusion that God has not been served from the beginning, that He has lost

The Current of Spirituality

interest, that there is nothing to be done to please Him at this late date, that the whole thing has been a delusion, and that the sooner prayer can be forgotten the better. Surely, God must prefer a more outward and active service, so how about the corporal works of mercy?

If that is how one reaches "defeat at the summit" there is good reason to follow through and see what kind of maturity might be found. A close look at the matter can reveal quite a different story. Tracing the attitude of mind back to the original intention, the first thing found is the desire to give. The offering was Abel's — the best of the flock. As time went on, body, heart, and soul passed into the possession of God. Body, heart, and soul belonged to God already, but God wanted them to be freely offered. By accepting them, God was not exercising a vengeful right or tricking a human soul into something which has not been bargained for: God was in fact paying the compliment of listening: the Creator taking the creature at his word. Had the soul been made aware of the true state of affairs, namely that the gift was pleasing God and that there was no question of failure, the whole thing would have been spoiled. The lesson was designed to be one in faith: to have been able to follow the process would have robbed the exercise of all point. "Blessed are they that have not seen but have believed."

The reason why lessons of faith are the most difficult to learn is to be found in the reliance that we place on feelings. We say that because we no longer feel full of faith

Failure

we have strayed from faith. One of the prime functions of spirituality is to substitute faith for feelings. Even when we know better, and even when we see it working in other people, we tend to bring our difficulties in prayer, in charity, in trust, to the bar of feeling. Fortunately we shall not be asked when we stand before the judgment seat of God what we have felt about religion, but what we have done about it. We shall not be examined on the emotion that enabled us to cry "Lord, Lord," but on what we did to fulfill God's will. It works the other way, too; we sometimes feel extremely sinful, extremely angry or lustful or unkind. The question is, how did we let those emotions express themselves? We may not have succeeded in controlling them, but did we try? The fact that we tried, that we wanted not to sin, will go in our favor. It is not how we felt about them, but what we did about them — how we exercised our faith.

It is by a curious inconsistency in his mental makeup that a man accepts the idea that courage is of a higher order more when he feels cowardly than when he feels brave, and steadfastness is more admirable in the man who always wants to quit than in the naturally steadfast — yet when it comes to religion and prayer he assumes that religious emotion is in some way meritorious and that prayerfulness is purely a matter of devotion. Spirituality is not sensibility but faith. Success and failure are to be gauged not by the degree of outward achievement nor by the feelings that they leave us with; rather they are to be measured by the degree of God's will which is to be found

The Current of Spirituality

in them.

How, in that case, does one know where God's will lies? One can be sure about nothing in the spiritual life, so how can one be sure that what seems to him a slackening-off, a manifest decline in fervor, is in fact an advance? At that point the spiritual adviser has to say, "Well, you see, the whole thing is a matter of faith." What else can he say? It happens to be true. As in all matters of faith, the only sensible course is to persevere. The substitution of one mode of assessment for another is bound to be unsatisfactory, unreal — an upside down Alice-through-the-looking-glass experience. (The explanation is not at all convincing to the person concerned, but it is worth knowing from the spiritual adviser's point of view.) A new language is being learned and the struggling soul is in a strange land. This makes for homesickness for the old country of facile devotion. His confusion is compounded when some of the foreign terms bear a likeness to the mother tongue but apparently have different meanings. The thing for a person in such a dilemma to do is to keep still and let the language develop itself. There is no quick breakthrough. The idiom takes time to form and is never completely mastered in this life. In the next life it will be simplified into "holy, holy, holy," but until then there will be difficulties of accent and construction — and always the sense of failure. "But I have learned in whatsoever state I am to be content therewith."

12

Actual Set Prayer

A genuine spiritual outlook, like prayer itself, is not something that one acquires straight off: as is the case with every habit, it grows with the act itself. The outlook and the act develop together, helping each other and extending their range beyond what is strictly religious. But spirituality has to be fed, and prayer has to be repeated; it is not a matter of making vague resolutions or addressing oneself at intervals to the demand of spirituality. In an age which makes much of the liberty of spirit, it may be thought that spirituality and the act of prayer require a discipline that is distasteful. But discipline is required. The supernatural view of life is a gift from God, but there is no reason to believe that it comes by a miracle: it has to be worked for like any other. Being able to pray is a gift from God, but if the gift is to lead to further gifts of the same kind there has to be

The Current of Spirituality

regularity, which means that there must be set times for prayer, and that they must be safeguarded as far as possible from interruption — otherwise one prays only when one feels like it, and that gets back to what was discussed in the preceding chapter: the need to disregard the play of feelings and to concentrate on the will and the work.

Spontaneity, therefore, is not the first requirement in prayer — much as we like to think of spiritual affection gushing up with bursts of original thought — but fidelity, by which is meant the calm, deliberate rendering of a debt. It means planning, seeing that you are not unnecessarily distracted, securing silence and a measure of solitude; dreary precautions perhaps, but interior prayer is not likely to be kept up without them. Granted that some sort of prayer-routine is decided upon, what happens next? Here books on the subject become either too specific, or else so imprecise and misty as to be of little practical use. What follows may not be of much help either, because only the Holy Spirit can teach prayer. If, however, the general approaches are indicated, and no more is attempted here, the encouragement will be to open up under the influence of grace and co-operate effectively in the work designed by God.

First, what interior prayer is not: it is not a secret or mysterious exchange with God to be practiced only by the initiated, the mentally equipped, the spiritually talented, the mature. All are beginners; the truths learned over the course of a lifetime of prayer are still the elementary truths

Actual Set Prayer

which were learned originally, but they are entered into more deeply. Talent, in the accepted sense of that word, has nothing to do with it nor, for that matter, has maturity. People's sensibilities become more attuned to the spirit as they practice prayer, and this will bring about a more mature and responsive awareness of the issues involved. But to be able to pray with the uncluttered mind of childhood more than outweighs whatever human maturity one might acquire along the way. To encourage those who find the prospect daunting, prayer should not be thought of as terribly time-consuming or self-regarding. Time is an important factor, but where necessity reduces the time which one should like to give to prayer, the grace of God comes in to make up the loss. As for introspection, the more Godward the prayer, the less interest there is in self. Ideally, prayer should be self-forgetting rather than self-revealing, for after all prayer is not meant to further the study of self — quite enough self-knowledge is revealed in the course of praying without one's having to dig for it. Self-knowledge seems to be more important, and more immediately interesting, than the act of prayer. When that happens, the focus is no longer on God but on self. Honesty is one of the preconditions of prayer.

Still considering the negative side, prayer is not a short cut to what the non-praying man has to work for. The work of the praying man goes ahead as industriously as anyone else's, in fact more so, because prayer is incompatible with laziness; but the praying man has the advantage of knowing that God is working with him and through him.

The Current of Spirituality

Neither is prayer a mark of clearance — a sign stamped on one's baggage by a customs official, giving permission to take ashore a piece of packed luggage. Prayer has to be something in its own right, having its own destination, and not something attached to something else. Jacob asked for a blessing, spuriously, and received one, but only because Isaac was blind. Neither can prayer be used as a bribe; still less can it be used as a threat: "I'll give up praying altogether, Lord, if you do not grant what I ask." God's arm is not to be twisted. Moreover, those who wish to be honestly prayerful will avoid setting time-limits to the granting of their requests: to do so is to put the emphasis on the subject's view of divine providence rather than on God's will itself. When St. Peter was in prison, neither he nor his friends asked that he should be released by a certain day. We are simply told that "earnest prayer was made for him to God by the church." He was released when God chose to release him; the prayer was one of trust, not one which looked at the calendar.

Now for the more positive aspects of prayer. As a starter, the first function of prayer is to give glory to God. That is often lost sight of in the wealth of petitions submitted to Him. It is not that petition is to be despised (there are four petitions in the Lord's Prayer), but rather than prayer is primarily praise, especially when it is remembered that prayer is directed to the One best qualified to grant requests: a prayer of petition is one of praise. A more direct form of worship is generally considered by the experts to be better, but in such an intimate matter as the

Actual Set Prayer

personal relationship of the soul with God in prayer, the subjective has its place, too. You would not benefit by forcing your prayer up the ladder to praise, which you would be doing badly, when you were being given the grace to express penitence or petition, which you might be doing well. A person has to take himself as he is and offer the kind of prayer he is given. It is no good praying at a level to which you have not attained, dreaming, say, of the kind of saint which you are not. Our Lord told the women at the well in Samaria that those who wanted to worship the Father would have to do so "in spirit and in truth." If that means anything, it means acting prayerfully but acting in true character.

People who reach up to the higher rungs of prayer before they are ready are lacking in humility and a sense of reality and are doing so more from aesthetic experimentalism than from the love of God. Like people who spend hours in front of the looking glass, they come to see themselves as they want to look and not as they really are, and so fall into a trap of their own making from which it is difficult for grace to drag them out. The truth is that nobody likes to be thought of as a pupil in the lowest class of the school. For the would-be spiritual man there is always the temptation to show spirituality *en belle tournure* which means so much modelling and posturing that there is little interest in taking the form which God means him to have. In regular prayer, and outside the times of prayer, the love of God should fill the whole mind and be the whole object of desire. Where images of oneself as a

The Current of Spirituality

man of prayer are allowed to hold, there is less room for the image and likeness of God which the soul is meant to reflect. The safest course is to be quite without pretensions; all can be left to the wisdom of God. The mansions of prayer may be all very well if one is writing a descriptive manual on the subject (as St. Teresa was), but they can too easily turn into a house-agent's illustrated booklet. Great houses are as dangerous as foreign shores, and are best left to God and to the people who belong to them.

The statement made above that the love of God should fill the whole mind during prayer does not refer to the mind's attention but to its desire. Attention falters, intention need not. What should be particularly avoided in prayer are the images which begin by distracting the attention and end by deflecting the desire. The images are mostly about oneself and about what a rare soul one is. The truly spiritual person, according to Ruysbroeck, "plunges into his nothingness without images ... in nothingness he sees all his works come to nothing for he is overwhelmed by the activity of God's immense love." What Adam of Perseigne calls the "spirit of fiction" (which gives us a technicolor self always riding Homeric situations with calm command) is apt to corrupt the whole range of our experience, but it is never more active than in prayer where the spirit of truth, inevitably less glamorous, often does not stand a chance. The ideal of an imageless prayer is set out in the *Philokalia* which describes the untrammelled mind as "presenting to God a formless and imageless memory, ready to receive nothing but impressions which come from Him

124

Actual Set Prayer

and by which He becomes manifest to it."

The purpose of prayer is not to amass a lot of information about God or about the spiritual life, but to get close to Him by the means which He provides — the spiritual life. "To know the Father, and Jesus Christ who He has sent." Jesus Christ is at once the way and the destination of the way; the spiritual life is the means by which He chooses to keep man firmly on that way and headed in the right direction. It must be repeated again and again that it is His doing and not man's. "You have not chosen me but I have chosen you": it is because we are capable of being penetrated by His knowledge and absorbed into His love that our response is possible. It is His knowledge that enables an answering flicker of spiritual intelligence in our heads; it is His love, which we are so anxious to call our own, that attracts us to Himself. It is because we are known to Him, and not because He is known to us, that we can find our true selves in Him. It is because we are loved by Him, and not because He is loved by us, that we are on the way at all.

In the course of giving praise and thanksgiving to God, and while expressing our sorrow for sin and making our requests, we are all the time strengthening the relationship between ourselves and God. That is precisely why spirituality is so important: we cannot afford to miss the creature's opportunity of identifying itself with its Creator, the sinner's opportunity of identifying himself with his Saviour. Seizing the opportunity is the act of prayer. It will be

The Current of Spirituality

objected that all of that is very fine but it does not teach us how to pray, what we have to do to seize the opportunity. "When you pray, thus shall you pray . . ." We can only build up on the Lord's Prayer. The pattern, basic to the needs of man and comprehensive of his expression and aspiration, is not so much a perfect prayer (it is that, too) as it is an *instruction on* prayer. "Thus shall you pray"; not "here is a prayer." Given the outline by God, man fills it in. Because man has to insert his own individual response, it is not of the least use for anyone else to hold his hand and do it for him, which accounts for the unsatisfactory nature of books which tell the reader how to pray. One might just as well tell the bird how to fly, or the baby how to walk. The bird learns to fly by flying, the baby to walk by walking, the man to pray by praying.

There is also the question of liturgical prayer, group activity in worship. Since man is by nature a social being, it is natural that he should pay homage to God in union with others. If his bent for private prayer receives justification in the Gospel where our Lord tells him that if he wants to pray he can go into his room and shut the door and worship his heavenly Father in secret, he also has the backing of our Lord's example in observing the liturgical feasts of the year and in fulfilling the requirements of the temple. Some see also in the text "Where two or three are gathered together in my Name, there am I in the midst of them" an invitation to pray in common. Certainly the Church has always been in favor of corporate prayer, giving its blessing only exceptionally to the solitary prayer of the

Actual Set Prayer

hermit; but even the hermit is encouraged, in the Christian tradition, to join his fellow man in prayer occasionally.

The neophyte will probably find that whereas in his private solitary prayer he was able to experience, at least off and on, a deep sense of God's presence, he now, reciting the psalms or singing hymns or merely being in close proximity with other worshippers, feels completely out of touch. He has to intensify his acts of faith and of love to make God's presence mean anything at all to him. He knows that enjoying the music and watching the ceremonial cannot be all that he has come for, and accordingly is likely to feel that he might as well be at a concert or a military parade. There is, however, the knowledge that self is less likely to side-track a prayer in which everyone is taking part than in the lonely prayer of the single worshipper. The difference between solitary prayer, the one that seems to be the movement of personal communication between self and God, and the prayer offered up in public is the difference between dropping a tennis ball on the floor and dropping a box of them. Apart from the question of bounce, it would be difficult to play a game of tennis with just one ball. Whether we like it or not, we belong to a set. There is a solidarity about the box.

If there is one mistake more common than others among the spiritually minded, it is that of imagining that once the habit of interiority has been acquired it runs itself. Nothing could be further from the truth. What happens to a musician who gives up practicing his instru-

The Current of Spirituality

ment, to the athlete who stops training — or more immediately to the churchgoer who does not go to church? The fact is that he cannot, from a feeling of security and superiority, scorn the tedious routines which brought about the habit. Nobody's spirituality is so safely built in that it will not come loose when neglected. It never does any good to look down upon the devotions of the humble, for that would imply that one belongs to the elect. "He throws down the powerful from their thrones, and exalts the humble."

13

Maturity

Sociologists tell us that maturity comes earlier than it used to, psychiatrists tell us that the lack of it is at the root of most mental disorders and that it may last a lifetime, parents try to delay it in their children, children pretend it is theirs and like to show off with it, educators base their treatment of the young in the light of it and yet have nothing much more to offer in the way of definition than comparisons (comparisons usually with themselves). So what spirituality reveals here is at least pertinent.

Self-awareness is often mistaken for maturity, whereas they are quite different things. Neither is sophistication to be thought of as maturity, nor being able to maintain the pose of being unshockable. Indeed, the ability to appear worldly and grown-up may in fact hide a basic immaturity.

The Current of Spirituality

It has nothing to do directly with being clever, though it has much to do with intelligently interpreting experience. It is something which evolves, usually as the result of being handled hardly by life, but sometimes by the mere passage of years, and is not something which, following a crisis in your life, you can make up your mind to possess from now on. "A man passes from adolescence to maturity," says Dr. Odier, "with a sense of autonomy, a feeling of interior value. But that does not happen overnight or automatically. A man has to know what responsibilities he is to assume as an adult, and he has to know what constitutes true value before he can deal with it. The adolescent may have to wait a long time after his twenty-first birthday before he comes to maturity.

The process of growing up is painful chiefly because so much of it is uncertain. People's reactions to situations are unpredictable, as are one's own, and nobody has certain standards to measure them by. One is constantly having to reassess one's valuations. The adult is better off: he knows roughly how to go about his assessing, and does not have to readjust his judgments every week. It is a mistake to conclude, though, that young people know nothing of life and that the old can congratulate themselves upon knowing all that they need to know. The young experience life in variety, the old in depth. In the end it comes to much the same, because while the young take less heed of life's lessons the old tend to forget what the lessons were. The sensible thing would be to start correlating them at an early age and then go on checking one's conclusions until one's

Maturity

declining years. The young feel more keenly than the old but are more able to discount their recent feelings in the discovery of new ones. What the young do not know (how can they?) is the way life works, the structure of it. The old, having witnessed the process of cause and effect, make more allowance for failure. The young see failure as accidental, avoidable, pretty much what is deserved if one does not take trouble; the old see it not only as part of the principle of life but as a considerable slice of it.

There is a curious fact about the youth-age confrontation: when in adult life a man finds he has let go of some aspect of truth which he possessed in his youth, he has to start looking for it again. If he does not do it he will not, paradoxically, grow up. His maturity depends on restoring a vision which was sacrificed to what was thought to be maturity but which was in fact an unreality. It happens not only in the case of spiritual values, but also in moral and social ones. Men trade justice for toughness, honesty for material success, friendship and kindness for power. The way back to these lost qualities is humiliating, but that is the price one has to pay. Maturity, even self-respect, may not be attained otherwise.

In the sense that we are considering it, maturity is the reaffirming of God's order in the creation of the human being. Integrity can never be wholly restored because the lesions, or scarred tissues, remain with a man even after he has been redeemed by Christ and made a son by adoption. Spiritual maturity represents something, however, of that

The Current of Spirituality

return to original wholeness which rational man was designed to enjoy.

That is the main reason why our Lord put before His disciples the ideal of childhood. "Unless you become as a little child you shall not enter the kingdom": you have to get back to that state which you once enjoyed when you were a willing subject and not a know-it-all rebel. We call it innocence, but a better word for it is simplicity, which has the added implication of singlemindedness, truth, and trust. It is the "single eye" which our Lord wants to find in His followers, the eye not held by a hundred other things. St. Paul is talking about the same thing when he speaks of God "choosing the foolish things to confound the wise." The simple beat the sophisticated every time. Those who are wise according to the wisdom of the world are apt to question too much, to rely too much upon their superior intellects, to attract the less well-informed to themselves — and be content with themselves instead of heading on towards truth itself. The foolish have nothing of themselves to boast about — they have no pretensions, but they are more mature because, like children, they are closer to the pattern laid down. It is better to be an honest-to-God cabbage than a plastic orchid; better, if it comes to that, than to be a real orchid giving itself airs.

The first innocence of childhood may be more attractive, but the second innocence of maturity is more impressive. It means that despite having trusted everybody only to find that trust misplaced, despite having offered love only

Maturity

to have it mistaken for something else, despite wanting to help and not being able to, wanting to get at the truth, and finding either lies or a truth more daunting than not knowing the truth, the man who is spiritually mature looks at the world, at life, at others as though his experience showed no bruises. The child, in growing to adolescence, learns to distinguish between those who can and those who cannot be safely entrusted with his affection. That is one of the sad things that we see in children: the tendency to calculate and, if necessary, back out. In the spiritual childhood there does not have to be the same qualified love; the spiritually mature have fewer reserves in their judgments than other men, and that is because they are more like our first parents before the fall, who had none at all.

With maturity inevitably goes the knowledge that one is nothing and that God is all. When they take comfort at all, the saints do so in the knowledge of their weakness, their helplessness. They know that when they see the depth of their weakness they have the strength of God to draw upon. When to us the saints sound extravagant in their expressions of self-abasement, it is only because they see more clearly than we do the futility of their own efforts and the emptiness of their own beings. Was it not an affectation on the part of St. Thomas Aquinas (we might think it was) to say at the end of his life that his work, that vast contribution to theology, was really nothing at all? Did St. Bonaventure honestly believe that the sum of all his learning lay in the crucifix which hung on the wall

The Current of Spirituality

of his cell? There was no exaggeration in either case. Knowledge humbles, and enormous knowledge humbles enormously. That is true of non-Christians as well: Socrates said, "I glory in the knowledge that I still do not know."

For us who are Christians, the only true maturity is life in Christ. That means waiting in Christ for His solution to the problems which vex us, and in the meantime exercising faith. We talk about the virtue of Christian patience, and feel we offend against it by being irritable when trains are not running on time, when meals are late, when people bore us, when sermons go on for too long, when the rain will not stop, when the mail does not come. Such occasions are merely opportunities for practice: spirituality undoubtedly helps us to put up with annoyances of every kind. Seen at its best, Christian patience is simply waiting upon God's will, and if one does it long enough he comes gradually to a mature spirituality. Problems which have to do with major issues of life, with life itself and death and waste and prayer, are never fully resolved: they have to be patiently endured in the belief that somehow there must be answers to those problems and that what is wanted of those who are troubled by them (and who is not?) is the willingness to be kept indefinitely in the dark about them.

In the industry of vine-growing and wine-making there are many rituals to be performed. The vineyards are sprayed, the clusters of grapes are wrapped in fine gauze, there is the gathering of the stuff into what looks like laundry baskets. The grapes have to be trodden on with

Maturity

much singing and dancing and instrumental accompaniment. There is the boiling process, followed by the sifting process, followed by the cooling process, followed by the process of pouring the liquid into barrels and bottles. Finally the wine is stored in a dark cellar. It settles and waits: sometimes, depending on the vintage and the nod of the expert, it waits for years. Necessary as the preliminary procedures are (and there is a moral tucked away in each of them if you care to look), the factor responsible for the maturing of the wine is the dull waiting in the dark cellar. Possibly a cheaper wine can dispense with some of the years spent underground in the vaults, the vintner's catacombs, but the wine which will claim jubilee quality must expect, uncomplainingly and in lonely stillness, to collect the dust. Delay is at the heart of Christian patience.

Nevertheless, to wait interminably for the will of God to happen is not necessarily virtuous. That was not meant in the illustration of the casks waiting to be rolled up into the light of day. Granted that waiting is an essential element in spirituality, trust, faith, and so on (in this sense the analogy applies without qualification) there is the indisputable fact that the will of God is being expressed all the time and does not have to be looked forward to as something to break the monotony. If the will of God stopped happening, man would cease to exist. (God, too, would cease to exist because His will is Himself.) One of the ways in which God's will declares itself is in putting upon the individual the responsibility of using his own will. Man must act freely, and choose his course of action, or he

The Current of Spirituality

ceases to fulfill his nature. For a man to say that he is now so completely selfless as to have no will of his own, as to be quite without the power to choose, is to pay no compliment to God. "A man," says St. Augustine, "is what he chooses." Let him choose God by all means, and stick to that choice as faithfully as he knows how, but let him not claim in the name of a higher liberty that all other choices have ceased to exist for him.

So man has to choose for himself, and if God means him to do that he must also mean that man is to make things happen. Man is given the gift of life and must so act that life goes on until God takes it away. There is no virtue in merely existing. God does not promise that life will be exciting, but He does mean it to go on, and that imposes upon man the obligation of pushing it along. If God means man to make things happen, the problem for man becomes one of choosing exactly *what* things. Choosing *how* to make them happen is another problem, but the answer to both problems is found in prayer more effectively than by any other means. Calculation as to "what there is in it for me" and "how can I reasonably pull it off" provides no lasting answer. These matters are short-termed, and though in the eyes of the world they show a veneer of maturity, spirituality does not give them a second look. When with the best intention a man makes the wrong thing happen, and does so in the wrong way, spirituality is not compromised in the least. That is exactly what spirituality allows for. Even when a man's selfishness makes him choose the wrong things, and the wrong way to get them,

Maturity

it is still God's will that the man should go on choosing freely; but spirituality will not survive long in a man who keeps to choices which he knows to be wrong. The question of freedom in relation to spirituality, particularly in the terms of maturity, requires a separate chapter.

14

Freedom

There must be many who wonder with sincerity and gratitude at what this generation has been spared in the way of medieval superstition; nevertheless, there are grounds for believing that the experience of the past seventeen hundred years cannot have been altogether misconstrued and misapplied. Perhaps if in our own generation we had prayed more we might have come up with a more convincing answer to the world's view of liberty, law, tradition and obedience. They all hang together but we do not see them as such because we do not pray enough: the Church pledges itself to those things, and spirituality sees them in relation to one another. In the providence of God we may indeed be at the start of a new era (let us hope we are), but freedom, for instance, must surely mean the same now as ever it did. True freedom is, for us, the ability to

The Current of Spirituality

live according to our Christian nature, as men obedient both to the law of God and to the demands of our Christian nature — our Christian constitution and tradition. It is not a question of sectarianism of this or that establishment, but of fidelity to type. The type in this instance is the type set by Christ, and fidelity to it is ensured by law. Indeed the Christ-type, which is the practical ideal for the Christian, is itself a law. It is the law of the Christian's nature.

"Every living organism," says St. Thomas Aquinas, "strains towards its own proper perfection." The vegetable strains towards its perfection as a vegetable, the puppy towards perfect doghood, the baby towards adolescence and thence towards perfect adulthood. It may be inferred that the unit in a healthily functioning organism (for instance, a nurse in a hospital) is moved by a vocational drive that pushes towards the heights. The drive may never reach its peak, but it is there, is deliberately fostered and, in a sense, is its own justification and fruition. That is true in the spiritual life, and one may assume that St. Thomas had the spiritual life chiefly in mind. The often quoted axiom, "Live according to what you are and you will grow," may be thought of as the enrichment of personality resulting from conforming to the nature of the subject, but along with it is freedom. The nature of every subject has its own laws, and to depart from them is to diminish and ultimately destroy the liberty of the subject.

John Steinbeck's great novel *Grapes of Wrath* opens

Freedom

with a scene at a remote country bus-stop where a young man, who has just come out of prison, is amusing himself by pushing about a small turtle that is on the ground at the side of the road. In the interest of its safety, he is trying to keep the turtle from steering a straight course across the road. The turtle refuses to alter its direction and obstinately pushes on as its instinct prompts. Reviewers have pointed out how the incident gives the theme of the whole book, which is about the refusal of a migrating family to give in to prevailing pressures. There may be a lesson too in the young man's freedom from prison which enables him to lead a far harder life among his family than he led when behind the bars. Tenacity, endurance, liberty: the fact is that members of every species must work out their own salvation in their own way, in the terms of the species to which they belong, and if they will not or cannot do it, they forfeit their membership, their right to truth, their liberty.

You do Christianity no service by lightening its appointed burden, its moral vision, and speeding up its pace so that it can run neck and neck with the world. We must have liberty within law, but heaven defend Christianity from emancipated turtles. The spiritual life teaches that those who give themselves to God are the truly free. At any moment they can give up their gift, and the extent to which they do so is the extent to which their freedom is limited. It is not unusual to come across interior souls who, in the hope of winning exterior souls, are persuaded to make concessions to the world which their spiritual natures

The Current of Spirituality

are unable to afford. That is happening a good deal today, when the need for evangelization in a secular society is great, but, unhappily, conciliation often becomes appeasement.

The liberty of the spiritual life is not designed to stand in competition with the liberty offered by the world. It is akin to the two kinds of peace mentioned by our Lord: His peace which He gives to us, and the world's peace. Ideally speaking, man ought to exercise his freedom of will by always choosing to act in accordance with the will of God. If he were to do so, he would not need a spirituality to tell him how to decide: by the law of the Spirit he would be always moved to follow his spiritual attraction. We know from experience, however, that we often fail to use our free will properly and therefore need the extra dimension of spirituality. Ideally speaking has come to mean practically speaking, and in practice we are so blind most of the time that we do not see the issues as they really are. Even given a reasonably sensitive and accurate conscience, we have to do a lot of guessing at God's will. That brings us back to our twofold need: a prayer-life which sharpens the blade of our duty, and a law to which our prayer-life refers us for confirmation. Without these two helps to our religion, there can be no true liberty, no true peace, no true certainty.

At this time in our history the religious man is taken to be the Good Samaritan, and the one who is heading towards the temple in order to pray is looked upon as a

Freedom

selfish introvert. The summons to Christian charity is as clear today as it has ever been, and the response to it is undoubted, but is not the response too often given in man's terms rather than in God's? Has not social service replaced supernatural service? Even where God is explicity brought into the work and made its final end, is not His immanence considered to be more important than His transcendence?

It would be wrong to think that what has just been said has no particular bearing upon the relationship between spirituality and freedom. We have seen that we are free only when we are being what we are meant to be. We have seen also that spirituality shows us what we are meant to be. We are free to be missionaries if we think that is what God asks of us; we are free to be contemplatives if we honestly think God wants that kind of life of us. St. Paul is full of the idea that there are divers functions in the Church but the same Spirit expressing Himself through all of them. Anyone who imagines that the Church forces us into a mold has the notion of the Church completely wrong, and has the Pauline conception of vocation completely wrong as well. Just as each vocation has its own responsibilities, each vocation has its own freedoms. Since vocation implies an election — the choosing of one kind of life in preference to any other — it involves equally a rejection. The married man, in choosing the state of matrimony, renounces the freedom proper to the monk, and *vice versa*.

The Current of Spirituality

A point which nobody has satisfactorily explained is why some people feel free whatever they do, and others who follow their light as well as they can feel perpetually constrained. Perhaps it is a matter of superficial reaction and natural temperament. There are those, for example, who can arrive at no peace until they have put their used bus tickets in the container marked unequivocally "Used Tickets," while there are others who lose not a moment's sleep after breaking every law in the Decalogue. Inexplicable as the human psyche is, and must ever remain, spirituality should be able to determine the balance. The man who prays should come to know roughly when he is acting according to God, and when he is simply being absurd. The spiritual life is not necessarily a substitute for good sense, but it should be a corrective to false piety. Good sense may or may not induce true liberty, but false piety will never get anywhere near it.

15

Work

It is not that Christians are lazier than non-Christians but that, having eternity constantly dangled before them, they tend to take their temporal tasks less seriously than they otherwise might do. The life of prayer should expose the fallacy of using the next life to hamstring the present one. If labor is a punishment laid upon fallen man, it is also an act of worship. Where the materialist sees drawbacks in labor, the man of prayer sees opportunities. It is not just a matter of hardship — the materialist trying to avoid it, and the man of prayer trying to supernaturalize it — but a matter of value. An aura surrounds labor; the man of prayer sees it, but the materialist does not. A well-worn phrase on the subject is "the dignity of labor," and writers, trade union leaders, shop foremen, party bosses, and industrialists make frequent use of it. There is, however, a

The Current of Spirituality

difference between using a slogan to serve one's own ends and using it because it expresses a principle. Modern man can benefit by it when he comes to see his work as a positive religious function in his life and not merely a necessary burden. He may benefit in the sense of using it as a distraction, as a form of self-realization, as promising promotion, as enabling him to move up the ladder socially and financially, but unless he sees it in relation to the final end of man the benefits are limited.

The distinction must be made between something which is a good in itself and something which is an end in itself. Work is a good in itself, but not an end in itself. All temporal ends relate in one way or another to the final end which is God. Even a good which may be called a good in itself is good only because there is something of God in it: in this life it may be enjoyed for the good that it is, for the goodness of God that it reflects. In this life, faith is needed to see it; in the next life, all the goodness which is known by faith to exist in the world, and of which we see only facets and dimly, will appear and be recognized in its proper setting. Prayer should show us where the goodness of work, love, beauty and truth really belong, where they came from, and where they must return. It is like hearing a tune whistled by a boy passing by on a bicycle and later hearing it played by a full-sized orchestra.

The goodness of work exists because of God and it should be seen as such. While we believe there will be no work, as we know it, in the next life, the goodness

Work

attached to it in our present existence is not merely temporal because of its place in eternity. With our minds always working in a time sequence, we think of values following one another as on a conveyor-belt: one good stops when another begins; but when a particular work comes to an end, the worth of it in the sight of God does not come to an end. You start, for instance, on a project for the love of God: you labor at it for months, perhaps for years, and through no fault of your own, it comes to nothing. Has your labor been wasted and the good evaporated? No. The good has survived, because the good was of God and God has survived. Far from being wasted, the labor has continued to gather value and merit from the day you began. The mere accident of the work not arriving at its fruition cannot nullify the value of what was put into it; the worth has been mounting up all along. Prayer has the effect of putting present happenings in eternal settings; by prayer, a man comes to see good in its ultimate end rather than in its present state. He comes to treat work with the respect that he gives to the act of worship, the act of love, the act of discovering and teaching truth.

To give us a practical example, our Lord worked: not only did He work Himself, at home and later (teaching is hard work), but He taught that man must work as long as he can and as well as he can. While a man's strength lasts, there is always the Christian duty of working, nor is it the Father's will that a man perform his work listlessly, ready on impulse to give it up, arguing himself out of it. There were reasons why an apostle moved from one city to

The Current of Spirituality

another, from one household to another, but no mention is made in the Scriptural account of anything that would excuse an apostle from being an apostle. Judas walked out, but he is not to be excused for doing so. Peter denied, Thomas doubted, all except John "departed and fled" right when our Lord would have most welcomed their presence, but they went on being apostles. Nothing in the Gospel text suggest that they took time off from their apostolate; they worked their way to the end, and some to the grace of martyrdom. Nor were their successors idle: Paul, Philip, Stephen — *Acts* tells us of their constant drive. It is as if the early disciples still heard, ringing in their ears, our Lord's words, "he that shall persevere to the end, he shall be saved."

While our modern Christian society does not lack drive, it does not have the same feeling about work. Work for souls is respected (more so now than twenty years ago, and that is good) but work in humble, monotonous, unromantic, dreary occupations is looked upon as an evil. It is not confined to an economic or class level; it goes from the factory floor ("I wouldn't be doing it if I didn't have to, but I've got to earn a living") to the highest paid Oscar winner who finds rehearsals irksome (and who says deprecatingly of a successful career, "I do it because I'm no good at anything else — it's just a job"); from the family living in a tenement and rebelling against the drudgery of their life to members of expensive clubs who live in fear of a strike that would force them to fend for themselves. The evidence suggests that, whatever it was like in society less

148

Work

urbanized than our own, we of a modern western culture need deliberately to orientate our work, to supernaturalize it, so that it gets back to what it was meant to be, to something of what it was in the Garden of Eden before the fall.

It has been said that work is natural to man. To me it does not seem to be that way. Natural to man are the desires to acquire knowledge, to see new places, to be amused, to swim and climb and ride; but is the desire to work a natural one? Perhaps once the work has been begun, and one has pushed oneself over the first hump, it is; experience shows that people who have never done a stroke of work all their lives often find, when for one reason or another work is forced upon them, a rare and unexpected happiness in it. In wartime the discovery of satisfaction in work is a common occurrence, but when peace comes the lesson is usually forgotten. If one is to judge by the psychological obstacles which often prevent people from giving work a try, however, there must be a special blessedness attached to it.

A psychiatrist probably could explain why the more competent a person is, the greater his resistance is apt to be. It is not only a subconscious reaction; even consciously, one wants to avoid being tied down to something. When one of the greatest living violinists injured his right arm as a young man, and there was the possibility of amputation, on being warned of what the operation might mean his thought was, "Thank God, then I won't have to play any

The Current of Spirituality

more." Unless he was the exception, and many of us have felt the same reaction about our own lesser talents, it hardly bears out the theory that work is natural to us. Therapeutic it may be, and it may lend a glow of very real pleasure when it happens to be something that suits our capability; but normally natural to us it is not. There are few satisfactions equal to that of having rounded off a difficult assignment, but that feeling is retrospective, and not inherent in the job itself. Furthermore, it has nothing to do with spirituality.

A point about work, and one which has slightly more bearing upon spirituality, is one which arises out of the perfectionist syndrome. The line from St. Thomas Aquinas quoted on an earlier page about "every organism straining towards its proper perfection" may be recalled. The "straining," encouraging in most of its aspects, is not an unmixed blessing. One of the consequences, for instance, is that the more you know about any particular work, the better you see its pitfalls. You also see more ways that it might be done — and done better than before. In wanting to do a thing perfectly, you are answering a particular human need inside yourself. In wanting to do it perfectly for the love of God, you are still answering a need inside yourself, but now the supernatural has been explicitly added to the natural, has indeed been claimed for the natural, and accordingly carries with it an added responsibility — and an added grace.

Compare for a moment communicating with God in

Work

work and communicating with God in prayer. In the life of prayer the temptation is, as we have seen, to doubt the validity of the summons, to become discouraged at the slow rate of progress, to give up. In the case of work the temptation, as you would expect, comes from without, but it is a temptation to lower the standard of perfection. The man of prayer may keep up a front, observe the routines of prayer, but no longer operate interiorly; the one who is looking for perfection in his work can also hide behind a front while ceasing to follow his ideal. In his case there are many more external factors which incline him in that direction. He is appealed to by friends, he is offered a reward for quick service, he knows he can satisfy his customers or his public or his critics by a facile display of talent and a slapdash performance which will take in everybody but himself and God.

It is, therefore, not only the prayer-man who shows one self to the world while he is another before God; the work-man, unless he is careful, does it also, and for the work-man there is a greater excuse. Many an honest craftsman has been lured away from his proper bent, not by the thought of gain, but simply by the desire to please. Men of great talent, and therefore of great responsibility, have been lured away from artistic and spiritual perfection not by the thought of publicity, but, again, by the desire to please. It must be the spiritual life which plots the course. Once give up trying to know God's will, which is what spirituality is all about, and you lose your bearings. Given the spiritual point of view, you should not have

The Current of Spirituality

much difficulty in seeing where the desire to please stops being charity and becomes self-advertisement. If expertise is the enemy of the painstaking individual, self-advertisement is the enemy of the perfectionist. Work far more often becomes slipshod because of vanity than because there is not enough time to do it properly or because of economic, parochial, domestic or technological pressures.

In our materialist society we are driven by what is prettily called the "productivity escalation" to judge by output rather than content or intrinsic worth. That viewpoint immediately makes the spiritual one less easy to understand; in fact, it makes the spiritual point of view look nonsensical. In the materialist concept of life, the only values worth bothering about are those which are effective, and which can be seen to be effective. That concept creates gulfs which did not exist in the ages of faith. The most obvious gulf is the one between the inwardness and outwardness of the work, between intention and achievement, between essential merit and demerit. There is also a widening gulf between work and leisure, partly because of the conditions in which people live today (their place of work being separated from their homes, in contrast to an earlier age when it was usually on their doorsteps and in some cases in the home itself) and partly because industrialization tends increasingly to become impersonal, mechanical, and boring, and jobs are sought for their incidental advantages more than their inherent appeal. A man is less likely to strike roots in a factory than he would in a smithy, less likely to feel at home in an office than on a farm, even

Work

working for someone else. That is not a romantic fancy; it is a fact borne out by figures which show that people do not strike roots in factories and offices but tend to drift from one job to another looking, reasonably enough, for higher pay. They are not to be blamed. When people seek jobs not because of any intrinsic merit in the work, but because of the salary and the holidays, it is not much good talking to them about the sacredness of labor.

The ideological gap is harder to bridge than the gap between spirituality and economics, the reason being that a cause can be identified with the Gospel, and consequently the existence of a gap is not admitted. The mistake is the more understandable because we are brought up nowadays to think by slogans and not by brain effort. A modern man may seek a job, not for what it is, but for what it stands for; when that happens the perfectionist is replaced by the propagandist. Whatever the ethical build-up, works produced without a spiritual motive to give them direction and destination are products of salesmanship. Outside the spiritual dimension which gives them substance, the fruits of toil are (and what a revealing term it is) consumer goods.

We saw in the case of fraternal charity that people must be loved for themselves, but with a further eye on God; we see in the case of work that jobs must be undertaken for themselves, but again with a further eye on God. Once that principle is admitted, whether with refererice to people or occupations, one is justified in accepting the satisfaction afforded. If he is going to do a thing well, a man needs to

The Current of Spirituality

find pleasure in what he does; he cannot love others without some sort of return. What we must avoid in either instance is leaving God out. The spiritual life teaches him that God blesses only His own loves, only His own works. When the creature excludes the Creator, the love becomes lust and the labor serves only venal, ambitious, or partisan ends.

16

Renewal

The problem of renewal is as great now as it was in other periods of Christian crisis, but we do not seem to have men and women who can solve it. Since we cannot know what is going on in the hidden lives of souls scattered about Christendom, we will do better to lay the foundations of some sort of holiness in our own souls. That is the only renewal that concerns us as private individuals, and even here we cannot be sure of measuring the extent of it.

We are given our cue in the already-quoted saying of our Lord: "For them do I sanctify myself." Though He Himself had no need to renew, He gave out His sanctification so that mankind might be renewed, and in that we are expected to imitate Him. We are not required to demonstrate holiness; we are required, even if nobody notices, to

The Current of Spirituality

reflect it. Christian renewal is the renewing of Christ's image in us. This is true of the individual and it is true of the Church: renewal is representation — *re-presentation.* Individually and collectively we echo the Word, the *logos,* but the Word goes on speaking truth, and the echoes go on vibrating the sound of it. Even truth, which we tend to think of as monumental, does not stand still. It unfolds, revealing more of itself as time goes on. The truth can never be taken for granted as the sum of all that can be revealed to man. We cannot say, "Truth made itself known, as much of it as was necessary to human life, and on a certain date stopped. If we are in doubt about it at any time, we have to go back behind that certain date and look for an answer there."

It is difficult to renew the letter of truth; it is far more difficult to renew its spirit. Truth is not something that we discover and from then on wear as a badge which can be pinned on to every suit we possess, and worn without a further thought. "I'm a witness, am I not? Look at my badge." Awareness of truth must be renewed every day, and with the renewal must go the decision to live according to truth. We have our model in the living Christ — not a dead Christ, but the living one. Renewal for the Christian means answering His summons. The summons comes in different forms, but, to quote from *Mere Christianity,* by C. S. Lewis, it amounts to this: "Christ says, give me all. I don't want so much of your money and so much of your work: I want you. Hand over the whole natural self . . . I will give you a new self instead. In fact I will give you

Renewal

myself: my own will shall become yours." A *new* self, a self re-newed in Christ who is forever new, is promised.

In the Jerusalem of our Lord's time there was much talk of renewal. The Pharisees wanted to renew Judaism by getting back to the primitive interpretation of the Mosaic Law; the Sadducees wanted the renewal to adapt Judaism to the contemporary culture, to the modern world where Greek and Latin were spoken. (Our present-day situation, with its conservative-progressive wrangles, is similar, needing only the transposition of two or three words.) It is significant that our Lord aligned Himself with neither party. The Pharisees tried to get Him to commit Himself to the code of their ancestors, the Sadducees tried to canvass Him for a liveral vote, but our Lord brushed partisan stuff aside and taught instead a spiritual rebirth. While the Levitical priesthood looked for a dramatic Messianic intervention, and the Zealots looked for a switch-over to Rome and Greece, our Lord went on laying the foundations of true spirituality. The argument was that, however explosive the political outlook (and it was to become increasingly so), the Christian's first concern was to address himself to the Father's will. It was not Christ's way to exchange one party spirit for another, to replace a conservative sectarianism with a progressive sectarianism: He taught that tradition has its place, that change has its place, and that only by responding to the day-to-day manifestation of the Father's will can we avoid the dangers which each presents.

Christianity is a pilgrim Church, peopled with strangers

The Current of Spirituality

and exiles; perhaps it is the sense of never quite belonging that we of this generation have lost. The abiding city offers all the advantages, and we have made ourselves snug in it. But is it the *civitas Dei,* the city of God which our early fathers sought? Is it not possible that with all the apparatus of travel at our disposal we have mistaken one kind of city for another, and that our need now is to renew our pilgrimage — and journey light? In answering the call to renewal we can blunder in any number of ways, but we can hardly go wrong in trying to return to simplicity — simplicity of spirit, but also simplicity of life. We can alter ecclesiastical structures, recast our institutions, direct ourselves towards new goals, brush up our theology, scrap our liturgy and use a different one, but none of it is going to lead us to renewal unless we acquire a simplicity of heart which everything in the world is doing its best to prevent. On the material plane, life is complicated beyond all reason (and we seem to like it better that way). Voluntary poverty is treated with reserve; comfort is assumed as part of the equipment necessary to life; luxury becomes a human right; and so it is difficult for religious simplicity to find a foothold. The mechanics of living have become so complex as to make down-to-earth Christianity such as the early Christians envisaged an almost impossible ideal Perhaps that is it: we have lost the gritty taste of simplicity. "Dust thou art and unto dust thou shalt return." Especially in the age of man's proudest achievements (we have, after all, reached the moon) we need to renew our humility.

In the literature of two ancient cultures, the Indian and

Renewal

the Chinese, we find an allegory which is substantially the same. It runs roughly this way: a flower looks down at the ground in which it grows and says to it: "Would you not prefer to be like me, pretty and graceful and waving this way and that in the breeze, instead of lying flat and drab all the time as you do?" "Yes, indeed," says the earth, and is drawn up through the roots to provide nourishment for the flower. Then a rabbit comes along and says to the flower: "Would you not prefer to be like me, able to run about and nibble at this and that, instead of being tied down to one spot?" "Yes, indeed," says the flower, and the rabbit eats the flower and hops away. Then a man meets the rabbit and says: "Would you not prefer to be tall and strong like me, able to stand upright on two legs and hold serious conversations with other intelligent human beings?" "Yes, indeed," says the rabbit, and the man kills, skins and cooks the rabbit, and eats it for his dinner. The story is told to suggest that man can come to be a little too proud of standing on his own two feet — tall and strong with his head in the sky and able to speak intelligently with his neighbor. Before claiming to be master of outer space, he will do well to remind himself of his earthly origins. He has not made much of a job of caring for his own planet, so there is still plenty for him to do here before he takes on other members of the galaxy.

The most spiritual family in the history of mankind drew much of its nourishment from the ground. Perhaps we do not pay enough respect to the earth: without it we would not exist. In one way or another, even processed

The Current of Spirituality

foods are derived from what comes out of the ground. Man adopts a rather superior attitude towards the vegetable, yet he has to rely upon it quite as much as he does upon the animal kingdom. Even the pagan ancients, for all their fanciful mythology, seem to have put a higher value on sheer soil than we do. Earth; the Mother Goddess; Pegasus, the winged horse, having to fly down from the sky every now and then to plant its hoofs on solid ground; Antaeus, renewing his strength every time his feet touched earth; Hercules, having accordingly to avoid a touch-down in his fight with the hero. This is not a plea to return to the spirit of classical legend (nothing could be more artificial), but it is a plea for renewal at the level of elemental human simplicity: Nazareth, John the Baptist, the Apostles.

How else than by exhibiting the detachment and simplicity of the Gospel can we draw attention to the practicality of the Gospel? We can talk about love and faith, but who is going to believe us unless we renew ourselves in all that goes with love and faith? If we are as pleasure-loving as the unbeliever, as exasperated when deprived of our luxuries, as reluctant (if not more so) to share in the hardships suffered by others, we are not doing much as witnesses to renewal; still less as witnesses to God. We know that ultimately charity must win the day, that it is the most convincing argument for Christianity, that there must be no reservations about it, that it must be the first point on which we start renewing. If we are honest, however, must we not admit that there are a lot of other things which we should like to try out before we start welcoming everybody with

Renewal

open arms? "It is not the poor, sick, and old I find it difficult to be kind to. Black people I usually prefer to my own kind. Getting on with people of other religions is no problem at all. In theory I love all mankind in Christ. It is ingratitude and lack of consideration I cannot endure. I waste my charity on people who do not appreciate it, who impose on me, who expect me to wait on them hand and foot and then show not the smallest thanks. I can forgive people who lie, who accuse me of things I have not done, who complain about the things I do. The people I find much harder to forgive are those who take advantage of me, who bore me for hours knowing that my search for Christian charity will not allow me to turn them away, who are always asking me to do things for them and who would be up in arms if I asked them to do something for me in return, who keep telling me how wonderful they are and how I should try to be more like them, who try to get things out of me by flattery or by making their difficulties sound much worse than they are: these are the people who poison the wells of charity for me." Yet they are just as much Christ's members as the others. The point about charity is that it is God, and that God is it, and that since God loves universally (and He must or He would not be God) charity must be extended universally. That brings us back to the simplicity of charity.

If renewal is to mean anything it must start with charity, include all the virtues with charity to interpret them, and end with charity. The reason for treating spirituality, simplicity, and charity under the one heading of

The Current of Spirituality

renewal is simply because a weak spirituality, combined with an indifference towards the Gospel summons to simplicity, blurs the vision. Preoccupied with material concerns, the soul has no attention to give. The needs of others, the need to renew, the need to distinguish between the necessary and the superfluous, the need to get down below the surface are all there, are even admitted to be there and to be crying out for attention, but the mind is occupied elsewhere and cannot properly recognize them.

The mood of renewal, as implied at the beginning of this chapter, will eventually give place to a mood of calm. In nature, in history and in individual human experience there is always a swing between contrasting manifestations. The tide comes in and goes out, the lungs breathe in and breathe out; we find expenditure and retrenchment, involvement and withdrawl, a slowing-down and a picking-up of pace. Today the pace in religion, as elsewhere, has quickened remarkably. Action is in demand, contemplation is not selling. But even in the renewal of action, there must be a corresponding renewal of contemplation. Without contemplation to send it on its way and in the right direction, action can only be a busy-ness, a noisy fussing, wheels going round but staying in the same place. It is a shortsighted policy to turn contemplation over to industry.

One of the depressing features of renewal is the way in which apostolic undertakings are set in motion at a frankly exterior level. The activist tends to be satisfied if an immediate end is gained, but that is not renewal; it is

Renewal

expediency. By definition intermediate means a stopping short, a second best, while the value of spirituality lies in its ability to look beyond the relative to the absolute and to be dissatisfied with compromise.

17

Summing Up

By way of gathering together the considerations put forward, I would like for the first time in these pages to record a personal experience. (Usually my books are full of them.) It had been raining, there was a full moon and it was summer; unable to sleep, I got out of bed and went for a walk. All along the road, which was unsurfaced and therefore dotted with puddles, were moons, hundreds of moons shining up from the ground. It struck me, the way things do when one is alone out-of-doors at night that all these moons, and millions more wherever there happened to be water or glass, were contained in the one moon — they were the work and property of one moon. I remembered how St. Benedict had seen the whole of creation in a single ball of light. I remembered also how a Chinese philosopher had expressed the same idea, and how I had

The Current of Spirituality

written down the quotation years ago but had probably lost it. The exercise of trying to recall the words, which kept eluding me, so occupied my mind that I cut short my walk, went indoors, and searched through a file of old notes. At about three in the morning, I found what I was looking for. The philosopher was Sen T'sen, and the words were: "When ten thousand things are viewed in their oneness we are able to return them, and we ourselves return with them, to their Origin, and there together we remain where we have always been."

You will say that this is what Blake put more shortly: "To see a world in a grain of sand, and eternity in an hour." Perhaps all poets and mystics are given to enjoy that perspective, some to hold it longer than others. It is certainly a perspective to be cultivated. In a world increasingly sold on multiplicity we need a vision of unity. Even the danger of over-simplifying the answer is not so bad as over-complicating the question. Religion in any case comes to us fragmented: there are doctrines to be believed, virtues to be acquired, prayers to be said; but as religion develops in us it increasingly should draw its separate activities into one. Just as faith, hope, and charity are felt to be aspects of the same movement towards God, so renewal, spirituality, communication, and maturity are felt to be actuations arising out of the same source and finding their way back to the same source — the source being always the Holy Spirit, the Spirit of the Father and of Christ.

Summing Up

Our knowledge of goodness, truth, beauty comes to us not so much fragmented as refracted. If our first and only view of an oar were as it lay half in and half out of the water, we would judge the blade to have been made at an angle from the rest of the oar. That is because objects entering obliquely from one element to another, each element being of different density, are not seen true. Some idea of the object is conveyed, but because one medium does not match the other, the idea is incomplete — the object is seen at an unnatural slant. Take the oar out of the water, or push it all the way in, and you see it in true perspective. Goodness, truth, and beauty belong essentially to God, but only glimpses of them are granted to man. Man sees them incompletely, refracted on account of the difference in element. The goodness which man sees in the world about him is not immediately associated with God. Truth seems to have standards of its own before it is seen as a facet of the divine nature. Beauty again, as seen in nature or art, is understood to be a reflection of divine beauty, absolute beauty, only when man has learned something of its source. Prayer, the response to grace, the desire to hand himself over to the service of God, the habit of living by faith rather than by sight and feeling — these things put a man into that element, the density of which is no longer alien to true perception. The divine attributes must necessarily, until the beatific vision is enjoyed, strike obliquely to the human mind. But by faith the human mind makes allowance for the angle of refraction.

The consequences are appreciated particularly in the

The Current of Spirituality

exercise of prayer, but also, though less emphatically, when the thought of almost any aspect of religion presents itself. In prayer we are drawn to greater simplicity and fewer specific acts. Outside the time of prayer the religious response is more direct, less diversified, and less troubled by scruples. The divine nature is exercising its attraction in unity: not one attribute after another, as through a many-sided lamp were revolving and shining upon the soul, but more as a single lamp conveying its light, though never fully in this life, in a single act. Granted the function of grace in this developing realization, it is always within one's power to help simplify it. There is no reason, for example, why our thoughts about the Church should be broken down in detail so as to form a scaled order of priorities. There is no reason why our thoughts about Scripture or dogma or Christian tradition should issue from our heads in the form of scientific analysis. Our aim should be to have the mind of Christ. Paul prayed for his readers that Christ be formed in them, that they should put on Christ, that they should walk in Christ, that they should die and rise again in Christ. That is simple, not a complicated program. Yet here we are, followers of Christ, forever speculating, questioning, splitting up, analyzing, codifying, labelling and card-indexing. If our prayer life were operating properly, we would be inclined to unity.

"Let this mind be in you which is Christ's." Do we let it? Have we, for example, the mind of Christ on current issues? Life would be far simpler, for ourselves and for those with whom we are associated, if we had. Instinctively

Summing Up

we should react to world affairs, as we should react to private and personal ones, not with "What is the general opinion?" or "How does it affect me?", but with "What is Christ's view of the matter?" and "How does Christ want me to act?" It is in the present tense that the questions are asked; not "What would Christ have said if this had happened in His lifetime?" but "What is His attitude now, today, towards apartheid, segregation, war, strikes, or whatever happens to be calling for a serious opinion?" We look to the press and the politician to give us a lead when the leadership of Christ is there for the asking. Christ, we know, is not consulted by postcard: if His wisdom is to be drawn upon, it must be in the communication of our prayer life, which is something that has to be built up; and the answers are not sudden illuminations. More often, they come in the form of a growing conviction, and even then they are not laid down as laws for others to follow. The moment a man looks upon himself as being in direct communication with God, and therefore thinks that he is an oracle empowered to direct in His name and command, he should know that he has got it all wrong and must start all over again. If Christ meant everything to a man, was his whole life, he would not assume a wiser-than-thou attitude and want to put people right on family planning, euthanasia, and what films were suitable for children. Unfortunately, for many Christ is hardly more than an extra person in their lives: someone to be met in church, to be invited to join the conversation when people ask about Him, to be looked to in times of crisis. Christ may be a reality to them, as much a reality as a television set which happens to

The Current of Spirituality

be in a room which they seldom use — the tubes are in good condition and the wire is plugged in. A good tube, however, is no better than a faulty one if it is not used, and the wire might just as well be a length of spaghetti for all the good it does to the screen.

"When ten thousand things are viewed in their one-ness ... we return to their Origin." For us, Christ is the unifying force, the centripetal energy at the heart of the world who "draws all things to Himself," the prime mover, the first cause and final end. In Him and by His light, man can come to see life and death as one. Joy and suffering, success and failure, the Church and the world, order and chaos, peace and persecution: all of them are understood in the one understanding of the incarnate Christ. The greatest blindness of our time is the inability to see the universality of Christ. From this lack of perception — a perception that should rightly be ours — must follow the failure to understand the universality of Christ's Church. Our danger as Christians is to imagine that the coming together of all Christian denominations is going to be the whole story. That coming together is, of course, a necessary step, but it is only the first one. We have never quite got it into our heads that Christ died for all, and at this very minute is living for all. Until we can see all men in Him, and Him in them, we shall be delaying His saving purpose. Incarnation, death, resurrection: by these great acts were the doors of heaven opened to the whole human race, doors which had been shut since the Fall. Our vocation as members of Christ is to help in "returning those ten thousand things viewed in their one-ness, together with ourselves, to our common Origin."